Diving Off
The Pedestal

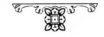

Demystifying the
Full-Time Ministry Mystique

Lila Joy Quezada

"This book is so refreshing! Weaving humor and insightful nuggets throughout her book, Lila's transparent sharing of her life encourages us back to the basics of who God is and what it is He wants from us. A definite must-read whether you're in the ministry or not."

Joy Tuggy—
wife of David Tuggy, translator for the *Nahuatl* people;
daughter of Cameron Townsend,
founder of *Wycliffe Bible Translators*

"This humorous and moving memoir is more than just another missionary story. This is an opportunity for readers to grapple honestly with the nature of professional ministry and the ways that God works through honest and humble people like Lila Joy Quezada. Before Lila was a successful missionary, mentor, and mother, she was my friend. 'Friend' might not top most spiritual gift lists, but it well describes the means by which God has used Lila to help build God's kingdom. There is encouragement here for all those who are wondering whether they could be used by God to reach the world."

Kenton C. Anderson—
author of *Choosing to Preach* (Zondervan 2006)

"I found this book delightful. The writing style is both witty and spiritually compelling. Far more than a biography of a family or individual, it is an expression of worship and gratitude, written with transparent honesty. It has a way of keeping the reader under a 'spell' until the last page is read. Every reader of this book will be blessed and challenged in his or her own spiritual sojourn with the Lord."

Vernon Middleton, Ph.D.—
Professor Emeritus of Missions, ACTS Seminaries,
Trinity Western University

"As a 22-year 'veteran' missionary, and mother of four MKs of my own, I found myself alternating chuckles and tears of recognition as I journeyed through Lila Joy Quezada's *Diving Off the Pedestal*. Any Christian workers who've been 'out there' will identify and be challenged to join Lila's dive off the 'super-Christian' pedestal into the turbulent, but infinitely more exciting waters of honesty and vulnerability."

Jeanette Windle—
author of *CrossFire, The DMZ, Firestorm,*
Parker Twins Series

"Lila Joy Quezada's *Diving Off the Pedestal: Demystifying the Full-Time Ministry Mystique* is an absolute delight to read. She invites you into her often challenging and even messy world, not primarily to tell her story but to use her story as a means to get a significant message across—that living on a pedestal as a full-time Christian worker is a sure path to disaster. I have to admit that it was hard to stop reading even when there were other pressing duties calling for my attention. The style is inviting, the story intriguing, and the message too important to ignore."

William Badke—
author of *The Hitchhiker's Guide to the Meaning of Everything* (Kregel Publications, 2005)

For Ellie, my husband and best friend.
Your love and faithfulness
help to keep my feet on the ground,
and your strong arms catch me when I fall.

And for our children:
Caleb, Joshua, Lucas, Isaac,
Johanna, Benjamin, Esther, and Lydia.
My life is incredibly rich and fun because of you.
I am so blessed and proud to be your mother,
and look forward to being the grandma of all your children.
Have lots!

CONTENTS

Acknowledgments

With special thanks to:

My son, Caleb, for your countless hours spent deciphering my chicken scratch and typing and formatting it into a recognizable form. ¡Que Dios te lo pague!

Jamie Loker, my dear friend, co-conspirator in countless endeavors, and grammatical nitpicker *par excellence*.

My mother, Euna Haynes, whose tireless prayers and ongoing affirmation have doubtless played a far larger part in this story than I will ever know.

John and Diana Lubeck, for your friendship and helpful editorial comments.

Joy Tuggy, whose raving enthusiasm for this book was all out of proportion to its merit.

Jeanette Windle, a successful author who took the time to offer invaluable advice to a stranger. I hope to meet you someday to thank you in person.

Elaine Wright Colvin, publisher and director of Writer's Information Network, who bought treats for my kids at Seattle South Center, and whose expert advice made me believe it could be done.

Ted and Pam Regentin, who lived through some difficult chapters with us, and whose wise cautions reassured us of your love.

Steve Beam, president of Missionary Ventures, who discerned something of value and was willing to invest in order to make it happen.

All of our prayer and financial supporters, whose gifts put food on our table and whose prayers give us the strength to go on.

An Invitation

As a missionary mum with over twenty years of experience in vocational Christian service, I am keenly aware that most spiritual leaders are not giants of faith. Pastors and missionaries are, for the most part, just ordinary people with wobbly faith whom God calls and equips to do a particular job. It is dangerous to pretend otherwise, because when respected leaders allow themselves to be elevated to 'super-Christian' status, painful disillusionment is inevitable.

Don't get me wrong...I'm not saying that Christian leaders shouldn't be honored at all. The Scripture is clear that those who minister should be held in high esteem (1 Thessalonians 5:12,13). My concern is that the appropriate respect shown to spiritual leaders can too easily degenerate into a form of idolatry.

The habit of elevating Christian leaders to a god-like status is, in my opinion, the cause of a myriad of problems — both for the 'pedestalizer' and the 'pedestalee.' No one can survive the upper heights for long, and the inevitable fall hurts everyone concerned. As an alternative to a nasty fall, I would like to invite my fellow Christian workers to deliberately *dive off* the pedestal by adopting a ministry lifestyle of honesty and vulnerability.

This book was born out of my painful experiences climbing up and falling off the pedestal. It is the story of how God graciously wooed me away from the desire to be pedestalized. Over time, I came to realize that the risk and the pain are just not worth it. It is my prayer that through heeding this challenge to authenticity, pastors, missionaries, and other Christian leaders might avoid some devastating snares. This is my attempt to 'dive off the pedestal'. Perhaps the lessons that God taught me might encourage you to take the plunge as well!

"He that is down need fear no fall,

He that is low, no pride;

He that is humble ever shall

Have God to be his guide."

~John Bunyan

CHAPTER ONE

A Friendship That Almost Bit the Dust

At the name of Jesus, every knee will bow,
in heaven and on earth
and under the earth, and every tongue confess
that Jesus Christ is Lord, to the glory of
God the Father.
Philippians 2:10,11

The tantalizing aroma of homemade tamales drifted in from the desert with the arrival of the little Mexican lady and her husband. But two pots of tamales were not their only contribution to the potluck. As they entered the house, an almost palpable tension wafted in with them, casting a pall over the entire group of missionaries and Mexican friends gathered there. This pleasant potluck luncheon was instantly transformed into an uncomfortable social disaster.

Unfortunately, it had everything to do with me, and all of our friends knew it. The Mexican lady was Josefina, who had been my best friend in Mexico for well over a year. She was my 'right-hand man' at the ladies' Bible study that I taught in Spanish. She was also my confidante, my most loyal defender, and a faithful interpreter of cultural anomalies facing me in our little Mexican town of Mitla, Oaxaca.

But now Josefina was totally rejecting my friendship! As she and her family walked in with their tamales, she coldly ignored me. Her husband, too, walked right past me, but deliberately turned his head away. Only her teenage daughter gave an almost imperceptible nod in my direction as she stalked by. No matter how hard I tried, none of them would respond to my friendly overtures. They cut me dead socially, and, insecure as I am, I was crushed.

Trying to busy myself with setting out food and pouring lemonade, my eyes were so blurred by tears that I couldn't see. When the tears started splashing onto the dishes, I ran for the safe haven of a side bedroom. After crying uncontrollably for half an hour, I finally gave up and made a dash for the car. Better to leave an intolerable situation in disgrace than to make everyone else miserable, too!

What had happened to sour such a wonderful friendship between Josefina and me? In retrospect I see that the culprit was what I refer to as 'pedestalization.' I had been a respected spiritual leader to Josefina—teaching the Bible study, counseling her and others, praying with her, and generally trying to be an encouraging friend. In return, she set me up on a pedestal and expected me always to be a spiritual giant.

Everything went okay until one month a kind of depression hit me. It was after about a year and a half of living in Oaxaca. All the little cross-cultural irritations that I could usually just brush away combined to dump their cumulative load on my spirit. No amount of talking, praying, or praising God succeeded in lifting the oppressive fog that I was under. I felt harassed by the constant stream of people through our little house, irritated by the extreme lack of privacy, and frustrated in my losing battle against the ever-present dirt and grime of Mexico. I was unable to express my discouragement to God, my family, or my friends. I didn't even understand it myself, so how could I expect anyone else to understand? I couldn't, so for a couple of weeks, I walked around in a melancholy silence, punctuated by frequent tears.

My family was baffled by my strange behavior, but never expecting perfection from me, they loved me anyway. Josefina, on the other hand, was devastated. Coming to my house, she met a sad and dreary missionary instead of her usual steady, cheerful friend. I fell off the pedestal that she had erected for me, and she was desperately hurt by my fall. Although I had never been rude or unkind, my obviously human weaknesses shattered the high esteem that she had previously had for me. She even thought that I was no longer a Christian. Obviously I was not a suitable friend anymore.

After the potluck fiasco, I was inconsolable over the apparent loss of my good friend. Seeing my grief, my husband confronted Josefina and her husband about their public rejection of me. They were contrite, but Josefina was still reeling in her disillusionment. Over the next two weeks, however, we took tentative steps to heal the breach between us. It was slow going because the hurt was so deep. Both of us shed copious tears, begged forgiveness of the other, and struggled to understand what had happened. She admitted that she had pedestalized me, and that she had never thought I could act in such an ungodly, self-pitying way. I tried to explain the phenomenon of 'culture-shock' (see Chapter Twelve), but it was all Greek to her. Over time, it was *God* who restored the unity between us, and His love covered over a multitude of sins.

The friendship between Josefina and me survived, but only by the grace of God. Sadly, other relationships tainted by pedestalization crash and burn. Look for trouble any time that someone assumes their pastor or missionary friend is above the petty weaknesses afflicting mere mortals. Every super-hero has a point of vulnerability—Superman's is kryptonite. Those of us in ministry are threatened by nothing quite so exotic as a trace mineral found in large quantities on another planet. Not being superheroes, our downfall can be triggered by nothing more than our own boring character deficiencies, absentmindedness, or plain ol' garden variety sin.

Pastors, missionaries, and other vocational Christian workers are often expected to have a closer connection with God, and to be 'a cut above' the average-Joe-Christian-in-the-pew. While it is true that Scripture sets high standards for those in leadership, it is wrong for anyone to assume that full-time Christian workers are exempt from the temptations and trials facing everyone else. If you are aspiring to Christian leadership, or already in full-time ministry, then you know the truth. You know as well as I do that we Christian leaders are just as prone to sin as the next guy.

Knowing ourselves the way we do, we should refuse to allow ourselves to be placed upon pedestals. Pedestal living is uncomfortable, lonely, and dangerous. If we go up there, we find ourselves prisoners of other peoples' expectations. With very little room to maneuver on a pedestal, it is terribly easy to fall off and to be dashed against the rocks of hypocrisy below.

There is a better option, however. Instead of just waiting to fall, we can choose to *dive off* any bothersome pedestals in our lives. We can regularly remind our friends and congrega-tions of our all-too-human flaws and foibles. We can humble ourselves, sharing truthfully about our struggles, doubts, and fears. In so doing, others will realize that those in ministry are just human, not perfect. Their sometimes unrealistic expectations of Christian workers will adjust accordingly.

CHAPTER TWO

God Chooses
Ordinary People

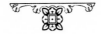

*Brothers, think of what you were when
you were called. Not many of you were
wise by human standards; not many
influential; not many were of noble birth.*
1 Corinthians 1:26

I was one of those rare kids with the special distinction of having *no* recognizable talents. While other kids spent their childhoods developing their skills and gifts, I spent mine moving from place to place. My dad is a professional forester, and our family followed an unstable logging industry around British Columbia and the world searching out jobs in all sorts of places. We moved thirty-three times that I can remember from when I was a young girl until I got married. I attended twelve different schools in my twelve years of elementary and secondary education. This extreme mobility was undoubtedly used by God to develop character in my siblings and me, but the short-term effect was that the only real talent it allowed me to develop was that of packing and unpacking. (Of course, that's a pretty useful ability for a missionary to develop, but I didn't know that at the time.)

I started piano lessons four times, but each time, after progressing a little, we moved, and in the next place that we lived we were either too broke for lessons or we didn't have a piano. Finally I gave up and didn't try piano anymore. In fact, I didn't try anything after that. What was the use?

It would be a mistake, however, to blame my lack of childhood skills-development solely on our financial and geographical circumstances. The truth is, I was also blessed with an amazing lack of manual dexterity and hand/eye coordination. I was the kid in Pioneer Girls' Club who could never finish the handcraft projects in the allotted time. After I would make a hopeless muddle of them, my friend Carol would try to bail me out by quickly finishing up my craft for me. Sometimes she succeeded. Other times I simply presented my mum with yet another unfinished potholder or mangled macaroni pencil holder.

When I reached high school, I couldn't sew a straight seam to save my life. My friends whipped out their Simplicity E-Z patterned blouses and dresses in two or three weeks. Me? Each project took me over four months to complete…and the results were pathetic to boot! (Plus, the same friend, Carol, had to help me finish — again.) Sewing was definitely not my thing.

Let's talk about typing. Somehow, while every other high-school student was diligently learning to type, I managed to squirm out of typing class because I was intimidated by the complexity of the typewriters. That did not bode well for me, as within a decade of my high-school graduation we were thrust into the computer age. So guess what? I am ashamed to admit that I still don't know how to type. In fact, I am writing this book with (gasp!) pen and paper.

One day when I was a teenager, I 'all alone bewailed my outcast state' to my mother. "Mum," I complained, "I can't *do* anything! Carol plays piano. Melanie figure-skates. Bonnie sings and she's in 4-H. Shari plays guitar, sings, and writes beautiful poetry. But I can't *do* anything. What am *I* good at?!" I could tell that my mother was desperately casting around in her mind for something encouraging to say to her hapless offspring. Finally she managed, "Why Lila, you're a good...friend."

Well, what was she supposed to say? "Why Lila, you're a good...vacuumer." Maybe she could have said, "You're a good hostess," if I hadn't recently dumped an entire plate of strawberry shortcake upside-down in our pastor's lap— desecrating his sacred Sunday suit! My lack of coordination was legendary among my friends who never let me live down the little incident of accidentally dumping my friend Melanie's beautifully decorated birthday cake upside-down on the floor. 'Grace' was not my middle name.

So I realized the truth. I had absolutely no marketable skills. The interesting thing about that realization was that it did not motivate me to get out there and develop some abilities. In fact, it had the opposite effect. I was like the Veggie Tales 'Pirates Who Don't Do Anything.' Spurred on by inertia, I stayed home and lay around. Since I loved to read, I lay around and read books!

Useless though that sounds, it was through reading that God caught my attention and directed me towards missions. We always had lots of missionary biographies and foreign missions paraphernalia at home—plenty of stuff to read. I was eleven years old, lying on the couch one day reading about Bible translators in Papua New Guinea, when suddenly it occurred to me that I, too, could and should be a missionary. That was it. That was my original 'call' to missions. Nothing spectacular—just a quiet sense that God had His hand on my life and wanted me to serve Him. From that time on, I had a general life purpose. Somehow, though, even that 'high calling' never translated in my mind into a drive to develop practical skills in order to fulfill that calling.

After bungling and procrastinating my way through high school, I was more or less ready for college. My parents encouraged my interest in missions, and suggested that I would need good training in the Bible as a foundation for whatever missionary service God might lead me into. With that in mind, I headed off to Multnomah Bible College in Portland, Oregon (then known as Multnomah School of the Bible). I knew that their motto was true: "If it's Bible you want, then you want Multnomah."

My lack of skills returned to haunt me throughout my college career, as I had to work my way through school. I couldn't exactly put 'good friend' on a job application now, could I? While other friends were earning six dollars a page for typing papers, I had no other recourse but to work in the school kitchen and dining room for three dollars an hour. Fortunately, or rather, providentially, I loved working in food service and enjoyed even such a low-paying job.

I found it a challenge to concentrate on my studies with all the social stimulation that a Christian college provides. In other words, it was hard to study while out on dates. Too many nice guys, too much fun! My freshman year found me doing several all-night cramming sessions to make up for a whole semester of neglected studies. I was exhausted.

It was a good thing that lack of finances delayed my return to Multnomah for a year after that. While I was nineteen, I worked as an office order clerk (no typing!) and also as a nanny for a dear family with six kids. During that year, God gave me the opportunity to go on two short-term mission trips to Mexico—confirming both my sense of God's call on my life towards ministry, and also my love for the Latin/ Spanish culture.

My junior year at Multnomah found me desperately trying to convince my then-current boyfriend to join me in my zeal for foreign missions. After an entire year of turbulence, we finally concluded that missions was *my* thing, not his. As we went our separate ways, I realized that no one can successfully manufacture a call to ministry in someone else's life. That is the job of the Holy Spirit alone. Had I known that, I would never have wasted my time, or his, in such a painful relationship.

As I entered my senior year I was prepared to avoid *all* men unless I was sure that they were going into the ministry. (This made for some funny conversations when turning down dates, let me tell you!) My friends were incredulous that I could be so fanatical and hard-nosed on this issue, but I had learned my lesson. Never again would I be caught in a relationship of conflicting life goals! Please understand that this account is intended to be descriptive, not prescriptive. In no way am I attempting to suggest that this is a formula that anyone should follow. It is just my story, which I tell in order to shed light on the very real struggles that I faced as an aspiring missionary.

Now I was in the right position for God to bring the man of His choice into my life. My handsome future husband was conspicuous as the only Hispanic guy on campus that year. I admired him from afar for his obvious love of Jesus, his strong leadership qualities, and his kind and friendly manner. I also felt drawn to him because of my love for Mexican people. Trouble was, whenever he stopped by for a cup of coffee while I was on duty in the dining room, I got all nervous and flustered. Instead of saying something witty and intelligent-sounding, I was more likely to spill the coffee on him—just me being true to form!

Apart from my complete lack of self-confidence around him, there was another little complication hindering the prospect of any real relationship with Ellie. Rumor had it that he was firmly committed to a lovely girl in California—in fact, so far as everyone knew, he was almost engaged.

Actually, although it was never confirmed, the assumption of his committed status eventually helped me to relax when Ellie came around. When he stopped by to chat, I convinced myself that he was just being his usual friendly self and was not actually interested in me. When he invited me to go get a Frosty at Wendy's, I was sure that he just felt like going for a walk, and I was the only person who happened to be nearby. However, as the days and weeks went by and our friendship deepened, I began to feel uncomfortable—like I was the 'other woman' in Ellie's life.

Finally I woke up to the realization that I liked him far more than was proper if he really did have a girlfriend. One evening, looking out over the soccer field, I told Ellie that I couldn't be friends and hang out with him anymore because I was becoming too emotionally attached. He seemed to accept that, and I went back to my dorm room broken-hearted over the loss of our friendship.

After spending a miserable night crying, I was shocked and confused when the very next day Ellie came by the dorm again asking for me. I launched into another explanation about my need to distance myself from him because I knew he already had a serious girlfriend. He interrupted my little speech by saying that there was no problem in that department, and then he went on to explain that it was already over with that girl. He was completely free to pursue a relationship with me, and he intended to do so.

My mind reeled. On the one hand, I was thrilled to know that this man I had unwittingly fallen in love with was deliberately choosing *me*! But on the other hand, I was now in the unenviable position of being seen as a 'boyfriend-stealing vixen' by others on campus who were ignorant of the facts. As our relationship became more obvious and I endured a few dirty looks from others, I couldn't help but wonder how on earth this had happened to innocent little ol' me. My greatest consolation was that deep down I was convinced that Ellie was the man I was meant by God to marry.

Far be it from me to let this steamy romance distract us from the overriding theme of this chapter. Getting back to the point, my lack of skills again reared its ugly head during our courtship. I was so impressed by how capable Ellie was in so many areas. He could play guitar, type, fix my car, run a chainsaw, lead chapel worship, etc. etc. (He had even sewn a dress for a former girlfriend!) I was intimidated as I watched the other girls type papers and bake pies for their boyfriends — things that I couldn't do. I became almost frantic searching for something practical that I could do for Ellie.

Knowing how foolish I felt about my lack of skills, Ellie finally suggested that perhaps I could sew a button on his suit jacket for him. I seized the opportunity (and the suit jacket), thinking that in this small way, perhaps I could prove to him that I wasn't completely incompetent. When Ellie came by to collect the jacket the next day, he commended me on what a good job I had done. "The button is sewn on so good and tight that it will never fall off," he said. Unfortunately, as he pointed out, I had inadvertently sewn it on in a spot where there wasn't even a buttonhole for it! Arrrgh! I was mortified. What had happened was that in the midst of my 'big sewing project' the night before, a girlfriend in need of counsel had dropped by my room to talk. As I earnestly listened to her problems, I had failed to line up the buttons with the stupid buttonholes, and the rest is history. I felt like a total failure — unable to do even such a simple thing as to sew on a button!

My lack of any discernible talent was puzzling to Ellie, but he loved me in spite of it. When he asked me to marry him, I joyfully said yes, knowing that God had knit our hearts together in love. We shared common values and the common goal of missionary service somewhere in Latin America.

Throughout our married life, Ellie's unconditional love has been a picture to me of God's love for us, His children. Ellie accepted me just as I was, and seemed able to overlook my basic ineptitude at just about everything. In the same way, God takes us just as we are without demanding extraordinary talent or exceptional ability.

It is essential to dispel the myth that pastors and missionaries must be derived from 'special stock.' People who habitually place Christian workers upon pedestals suppose that God only calls people of extraordinary family backgrounds, skills, and talents into full-time ministry. Nothing could be further from the truth—at least in my case.

Post-Pedestal Pondering

From my experience, we can conclude that the way to become qualified for service in God's Kingdom is *not* by:

- Our heritage

- Our skills and abilities

- Our physical coordination

- Our technological competence

- Our self-confidence

God's criteria for His servants are that we are forgiven, obedient, and available. When we willingly surrender our gifts (or lack thereof!) and ourselves to Him, He will begin to mold and shape all of our life experiences to His honor and glory!

CHAPTER THREE

Practically Perfect
Pedestal People

*Now I, Nebuchadnezzar, praise and exalt
and glorify the King of heaven, because
everything he does is right and all his ways
are just. And those who walk in pride he is
able to humble.*
Daniel 4:37

**Caution! This chapter is not for the faint of heart.
Reader discretion is advised.
The following account graphically illustrates that God is
unrelenting in His resistance of the proud.**

You might assume that my complete lack of marketable
skills would have psychologically hamstrung me from
pursuing a career in missions. You might assume that, but
you would be wrong. It wasn't that I believed that God uses
ordinary people, and so He could use me. No, I believed that

I was *extra*ordinary—merely undiscovered. You see, among my siblings and me there was a sort of 'reverse snobbery' in effect. The logic went something like this: "We are poor, and unskilled, and just sit around and read a lot, so therefore we are better than everyone else." I know, I know…it makes no sense. But that's what we sort of thought deep down inside. Go figure!

Illogical though it was, with that dynamic operating, once Ellie and I were married, I had visions of us being 'super-missionaries.' *I will come up with the ideas, and he will work with his hands and 'do the stuff.' Together we will make a wonderful team. In fact, just like Mary Poppins, we will be 'practically perfect.'* Looking back, I am amazed at the arrogance that I displayed. When we were accepted as short-term assistants with Wycliffe Bible Translators, I had to write up a little introductory blurb to go with our picture. This is what I wrote:

> *Ellie and Lila see their individual backgrounds*
> *as ideal preparation for a life of*
> *missionary service together*
> *… blah blah blah…*

Notice how revealing that first sentence was. With such ideal preparation, I implied, we will be the ideal missionary couple. The sad thing is that I truly believed it.

Sometimes it is the lay Christians who place full-time Christian workers up on a pedestal. In my case, I spared them the effort of hoisting us up, as I was only too eager to float up there myself. In other words, I elevated *us* to the position of *Practically Perfect Pedestal People*—or *PPPP*s. *Practically Perfect Pedestal People* have an inflated opinion of themselves, which raises them to super-status—at least in their own eyes.

Such was my state of mind as we headed off to Guatemala—
our first missionary assignment. Fresh out of Bible college,
newly married with a cute little baby boy, a smattering of
training in linguistics, literacy, and community development—
I mean, what was there not to like? Full of self-importance, I
was sure that we would do great. In fact, we would *be* great!

That was before the fall. Little did I realize how woefully
unprepared I was to be used by God while walking in such
pride and self-confidence.

Let me hasten to assure you that Ellie had no such delusions of grandeur. Humble and level-headed, he just wanted
to serve God. Since my delusions were mostly at a subconscious level, he was not aware of my unhealthy frame of
mind. To tell the truth, neither was I.

The trouble with *Practically Perfect Pedestal People* is
that, like Mary Poppins, they are just a figment of someone's
imagination. Like Mary Poppins, they do not really exist.
And like Mary Poppins, all it takes is a change in the wind
for them to disappear.

During our two years in Guatemala, God set about to
'change the wind' to make my *PPPP* ambitions disappear.
He doesn't need, nor does He want any *PPPP*s in His service,
so He systematically set out to destroy my grandiose visions.
It took one crushing blow after another until my sense of
failure was complete.

I remember when Ellie and I were sitting with our supervisor, Paul Townsend, in our adobe house in Chajul, the
Indian village where we were assigned to live and work. A
true visionary and a bundle of limitless physical energy, Paul
Townsend was accomplishing great things in the two language
areas that he was supervising. Not only was he translating
the New Testament, but he also organized literacy classes,
teacher-training programs, child-sponsorship programs, rural
pharmacies, pastors' conferences, home-hygiene classes,
relief and development programs—you name it, he did it!

"Now," Paul asked this newly-arrived rookie couple, "How do you see yourselves fitting into the big picture here? I need help with the administration of all these programs... can you help me?"

"Oh yes!" we confidently assured him. "We can help with *all* of the above!"

"And in addition," I stupidly chimed in, "I will hold Bible classes for the women and start a midwifery training program in my spare time!" (Me and my big mouth.)

Paul was delighted to know that help had arrived, and he returned to his translation duties in the city secure in the knowledge that Ellie and Lila, self-proclaimed *PPPP*s, were on the job.

Well, within a very few weeks, culture shock struck with a vengeance, paralyzing me for all intents and purposes. I was appalled by the primitive living conditions in Chajul, isolated by the language barrier, and weakened by amoebic dysentery. Not only that, but I was frantic to protect our one year-old son, Caleb, from the tuberculosis germs that were endemic to that area. The mortality rate was fifty percent for children under the age of five, which was not reassuring. It didn't help my state of mind when our new Indian friends would come to visit and nonchalantly spit on our floor—the very same floor where Caleb was playing!

Not surprisingly, we headed back to the city at the next available opportunity. Ostensibly it was to stock up on supplies, but the truth is that I was desperate for a reprieve from the rats, the germs, and the general filth. What had happened to my ideals of being a 'Super-Missionary' who could cope with any challenge?

It wasn't as if I could debrief by talking about my struggles with the veteran missionaries who were around. Hearing their experiences as pioneer missionaries back in the 1940s and '50s made me feel like an absolute wimp by comparison. *Who am I to complain about foot-long rats? They probably dealt with three-foot-long Rodents of Unusual Size 'back in their day!'* I wanted to appear as if I was adjusting just fine, thanks, so I bottled up my fears and pretended that, like them, I couldn't *wait* to get back to the village!

Words could not express my relief when a message came via two-way radio that there was a lot of guerrilla activity surrounding our village. Because of the fighting, it was not safe for us to attempt a return to the village until further notice. I pretended to bravely swallow my disappointment at the delay, but inwardly I dreaded the day when the violence would subside enough to permit our return.

Now let me ask you: does this sound like I was deeply concerned over the lost souls who might soon be facing an eternity without Christ? Nope. Did I care about those who might be killed in the fighting? Nope. I was just relieved that our little family could stay in the relative comfort of the city for a little while longer.

Of course, I never admitted my hypocrisy and lack of compassion—not even to myself. I still thought of us as *PPPP*s—we were simply facing some challenging circumstances settling in. That's when God had to start playing hardball with me to bring me to the end of my self-importance.

I'm afraid that things went from bad to worse. Ellie was valiantly struggling to fit into an administrative role that was way over his head and outside of his gifting, while I was usually sidelined by illness. I was already weakened and hospitalized with amoebic dysentery when we discovered that I was pregnant with our second child. Now I faced severe, debilitating, and unremitting nausea. Ellie was torn between tending to his duties in the village, and caring for a sickly wife and an active one-and-a-half year-old.

The one time that I attempted to travel back to the village with him during that first trimester of pregnancy ended as a disaster. I was sitting in the house, overcome by nausea, and I allowed Caleb to go play outside with the neighbor kids. A while later when I roused myself to go check on him, I found them all having a wonderful time…squishing human feces between their fingers like mud pies!

You see, at that time, the village of Chajul where we lived was much like a village during the Middle Ages. Standards of hygiene were almost non-existent, and latrines were few and far between. Our neighbors were like most of the other folks around—just doing their business out in the yard and leaving it there.

Needless to say, I was horror-struck as I grabbed Caleb, scrubbed his hands raw, and spent the next hour vomiting in our latrine. I was unable to control the vomiting after that, and in desperation Ellie called on Missionary Aviation Fellowship to come and fly Caleb and me back to the city right away. I felt sorry for our friend Ludín, the MAF pilot, as I vomited repeatedly and noisily all during the flight.

After that auspicious event, any lingering hopes that I cherished about 'accomplishing something great for God' flew right out the window. All I could manage to accomplish now was bare survival—and sometimes even that was in doubt. My mum flew to Guatemala from Canada for several weeks in an effort to keep me from starving to death during this pregnancy. She cooked up tasty and familiar dishes to try to tempt my palate. I would force myself to eat what she served, but more often than not lost it afterwards. She patiently nursed me through what we thought were the worst weeks, and then she had to return to Canada.

But the downward spiral continued. Next I started bleeding and cramping—a threatened miscarriage. In an attempt to stop the symptoms, I took a medicine the doctor had prescribed, only later to discover that it was actually an arthritis medication that was contraindicated during pregnancy. I felt angry and frustrated that the drugs that were supposed to help my unborn baby survive had only further threatened his life.

At a very low point, when I had almost given up hope for my baby's life, my cousins in Canada offered to fly me home to receive medical attention there. Ellie agreed that it was time to get help, and he put Caleb and me on the very next available flight.

It was not exactly a triumphal return to the homeland—barely one year from when I had so confidently set out. In fact, it was humiliating. Still, for my baby's sake, I was grateful for the help, and during the six weeks home I made steady improvement. When baby and I were both definitely out of the woods, Caleb and I flew back to Ellie's waiting arms.

Now five months along and over the nausea, I took another stab at adjusting to life in the village of Chajul. I don't know...maybe I made a bit of progress, but I looked forward to the 'six week policy' that would very soon go into effect and we would return to the city. Our mission had a policy that expectant mums were not supposed to remain out in remote allocations past six weeks before their due date. It was a wise policy, but again I was secretly glad for any excuse—especially an 'official' one—not to be in the village.

The glad day of baby's birth came and all my fears for this child's health proved to be unfounded. Josh was a bouncing baby boy, and when I say bouncing, I do mean bouncing! He was the fattest, rolly-polliest baby anyone had ever seen! After I had regained my strength, we headed back to Chajul where the Indian people thought he was some kind of freak. The ladies in Chajul nursed their babies, as I was doing, but also supplemented mother's milk with coffee made from unboiled water. Predictably, their babies often died, and those that survived never thrived as Josh was obviously doing.

We enjoyed a brief period of relative productivity in the village, and I cherished the hope that maybe now we could prove ourselves to be *PPPP*s. That was before the hepatitis struck.

When Josh was two months old, I came down with the classic symptoms of hepatitis—yellow eyes, jaundiced skin, and other nasty stuff. I couldn't believe it—after all the health challenges that I had survived, now I was facing several weeks of enforced bed rest. It was like a bad dream. I felt so guilty for again keeping Ellie away from his other duties as he struggled to care for a bedridden wife, a two-year-old child and an infant. Now I see that God in His mercy wouldn't let any of my secret ambitions of glory remain. He just kept turning the thumbscrews.

After spending Christmas in the city (with me mostly in bed!) we judged that my bilirubin count was sufficiently normal to allow at least Ellie to return to Chajul. I could make do on my own for a couple of weeks—as long as I took it easy. By this time, Ellie was desperate to get back to work. Even I was eager to go back to our village assignment as soon as possible, in order to prove that we weren't entirely useless. But naturally, we jumped the gun.

On Day Twelve in Chajul, Ellie, too, came down with hepatitis. Somehow he made it back to the city lying in the back of a pickup truck, sicker than he had ever been in his life. I received him warmly with a gleeful laugh and comforting little gems such as "Oh good! Now you know what it's like for me to be pregnant and sick!" and "I'm so glad you're nauseated. Now you can understand!" Compassion is not my strong suit.

I should have held my tongue, though, because within a couple of days my bilirubin levels went wacko again, and I found myself back in bed with a full-blown relapse! Ellie and I spent January, February, and March basically bed-ridden while trying to entertain our two little boys. Life was not fun. But it got even worse.

As Ellie and I gradually emerged from our cocoons of illness, it was only to watch in horror as Caleb started to exhibit mysterious symptoms of his own. Caleb's hepatitis was easy to identify and it was a very mild case, but other symptoms had us completely bewildered. Although he was eating well, his hair started falling out in clumps until he was mostly bald in places. His skin was covered in an unidentifiable rash that itched like crazy and soon developed into painful sores. We dragged Caleb from doctor to doctor seeking a treatment to cure him and finding none. As each doctor experimented with different medications, we held our breath hoping and praying that maybe *this* drug would be the solution.

In between treatments, we attempted to return to life in Chajul, but those trips were also short-lived. Caleb was in an agony of itching, and we had to wrap his bleeding feet and legs in wet towels at night just to buy him a couple of hours of rest.

It didn't help the situation that the area of Chajul was again plagued by guerrilla warfare. Soldiers with machine guns routinely came to our house asking Ellie to transport their wounded buddies to the hospital in nearby Nebaj. The military base was just below our house, and we used to walk down the path to watch the army helicopters strafing the hills for unseen guerilla warriors hiding in the cornfields. Ellie and I were fascinated by all of this military activity. It never occurred to us at the time that three-year-old Caleb was being traumatized by it all.

Eventually, however, in the interest of safety and in desperation to help Caleb, we returned to the city. Although we continued to seek medical help, it was a fruitless search. Nothing helped, and Caleb only got worse. Some friends suggested that perhaps it was a demonic attack necessitating spiritual warfare. Though we really didn't know much about that topic back then, we called together several friends to pray over Caleb. People claimed healing for him in Jesus' name, and we were filled with hope that maybe it would be a miraculous and instantaneous healing. But that was not to be.

Now, as any parent knows, it is one thing to suffer yourself, but it is another thing entirely to watch your child suffer.

Ellie and I could only stand by and watch in agony as Caleb's condition continued to deteriorate. I was convinced that he had something horrible like leukemia, and I was frantic to get him good medical attention. By this time, any ambitions of making a significant contribution in Chajul were long gone. My only concern now was to save the life of my child.

It was at this time that we received news that my parents back in Canada had separated after thirty-three years of marriage. That was the final straw that God allowed to be loaded onto my breaking back. Already panicked about Caleb, I was now consumed with grief and concern for my parents as well.

Finally, Ellie and I met with our mission directors, and they agreed that we needed to return home for a while, both to seek medical help for Caleb and to seek counseling for me.

The fall was now complete. Arriving back in Canada, I felt like an utter failure. For two years I had served as a missionary on an exotic foreign field and I had accomplished absolutely *nothing* of eternal value. I had no glowing success stories to report back to our churches, and in my shame I didn't even want to go to church.

Around that time, someone asked me what was the main lesson I had learned during our time in Guatemala. Devastated as I was by my failure to live up to the imagined *PPPP* status, I answered, "The most important lesson is this: When you need to close a plastic garbage bag, and you can't find a handy twisty tie, you can just grab two corners of the bag, twist them and then tie them together. *Voila!* The garbage bag is closed."

Now obviously I was being facetious, and obviously I had learned other more valuable lessons than that, but I couldn't think of any at the time.

God had effectively changed the wind and forced His poor little daughter to recognize her uselessness while masquerading as a *PPPP*. He shattered my pride, but only to bind up my wounds. He bruised me, but only to heal.

Post-Pedestal Pondering

Pride always causes problems. I know now that when we, as Christian workers, indulge in pride, we invite disaster. I hope that through this painful account you can see that pride:

- Prevents usefulness in God's service

- Invites disaster

- Cancels compassion for others

- Will be opposed by God Almighty

- Is never profitable

If you are walking in pride and self-confidence, your ministry will not survive. No matter how high you may be tempted to exalt yourself, God is ready and able to humble you. Take my advice (and that of someone in the Bible named Peter): Humble _yourself_ under the mighty hand of God…before He is forced to do the job for you!

CHAPTER FOUR

Picking Up the Pieces

Come, let us return to the Lord. He has torn us to pieces,
but he will heal us; he has injured us
but he will bind up our wounds.
Hosea 6:1

So, there I was, back in Canada with my deflated ego, my decimated family of origin, and my desperately sick little boy. (Always avoid alliteration!)

Ellie, strong and supportive as always, lovingly tried to encourage me as I struggled to make some sense out of my shattered dreams. He himself was disappointed with our "missionary performance," but he was by no means devastated. *That is all very well for him*, I thought, *but he hadn't expected to be a missionary of epic proportions. He didn't have so far to fall.*

Our first priority was to get medical help for Caleb. His symptoms baffled even the Canadian doctors who ran tests and at least eliminated the most deadly scenarios. No matter what treatment he received, however, he failed to improve and sometimes even got worse! One of the medications prescribed by a noted skin specialist did such damage that we had to rush Caleb to the hospital emergency room. Throughout this ordeal, we continued to seek out prayer warriors who could do spiritual battle over our young son, and we ourselves cried out to God to have mercy on his little body. Still no change.

It wasn't until I began counseling with a Christian counselor that some light was finally shed on Caleb's condition. In a show of support, Ellie usually accompanied me to my counseling sessions, and the counselor was reassured by our solid marriage. One day, though, he asked us to bring Caleb in with us for a visit. After chatting with Caleb, and observing our family interaction, he had some incredible insights.

What he noticed was that Caleb was exhibiting obsessive-compulsive behavior. Our little three-year-old boy would 'freak out' if his shirt wasn't tucked in perfectly or if his shoelaces weren't exactly evenly matched. The counselor observed: "Caleb is obsessing over the little details in his world, because the big things are so obviously out of control. All the instability of your lives, the violence around the village, and the prolonged illness of his parents have traumatized him. His immune system is totally broken down by the stress levels that he is experiencing, and he is taking his stress cues from you, Lila."

The counselor warned us that there was no medical cure for Caleb's condition and that the only thing that would help him would be to create a structured, stable environment where he could feel safe. "Establish predictable routines and make Caleb's world orderly," he told us. "Eat meals at the same time, go for a walk every day after breakfast, put him down for a nap *in the same bed* every day, and read him bedtime stories." In a word—*security.*

We were stricken as we considered that Caleb's suffering was largely parent-induced. Even in the midst of our travels and tribulations, we could have created a more stable environment for him. We could have prevented much of his stress—not all of it, of course, but maybe enough to keep his immune system intact. We felt like child abusers who inflict suffering on their own children. Though it was hard to swallow, the counselor's diagnosis rang true. But how could we fill his prescription?

Our plan was to return to Guatemala after three months. The counselor said that I only needed six or seven weeks of counseling to get my head together, and we did try to help my parents reconcile, but to no avail. Therefore we expected to return to Guatemala promptly, pending an improvement in Caleb's health. But how could we return to the very same conditions that had so devastated him?

We decided to request a city assignment that would hopefully allow us to achieve a measure of stability for Caleb. For a super-missionary wannabe, that in itself was a hard decision to come to. *It feels like we are admitting that we can't quite make the grade—that the village of Chajul has defeated us.* To a certain extent it seemed that we were being irresponsible, going back on our word, and neglecting our duty if we didn't persevere in Chajul. Not that we had been what could be called a 'smashing success' in our village assignment. 'Dismal failure' were the words that sprang to *my* mind. Nevertheless, in requesting a city assignment, I still felt that we were letting our mission down.

Weeks passed as we negotiated with our mission directors and considered various city assignments. Nothing seemed tailored to fit, and finally we concluded that God was gently closing the door to Guatemala for us at this time. After all we had been through, I should have been relieved, but I wasn't. I loved Guatemala (though not Chajul!), and I truly wanted to return. Plus, from the time I was eleven years old, my whole identity had revolved around being a 'foreign missionary.' If that was taken away from me, then who was I?

I think it was in my last week of counseling that I was wrestling with this issue. The counselor suggested that I ask my husband what it was that *he* wanted to accomplish in his lifetime. My first response was "Duhh…like I don't already know! He wants to be a missionary, of course!"

Still, the counselor urged me to ask him, so traveling home that day on the Fort Langley ferry, I said, "Ellie, when you come to the end of your life, what do you want to be able to say that you have accomplished?"

Ellie responded, "Well, I want to be able to say that I was a good husband and a good daddy."

"Yeah, yeah, of course you do, but what else is it that you really want to achieve?" I asked.

He replied, "Well, I want to have been a good husband and a good daddy."

I was frustrated at his seeming inability to grasp such a simple question, and so I tried again. "I know that you want to be a good husband and a good daddy, but *besides* that, are you planning to start a new mission, or do you hope to find a cure for world hunger…or what is it that you really want to do?"

His answer absolutely floored me: "Lila, at the end of my life, I don't care about anything else. I just want to be able to look back and know that I was a good husband to you and a good daddy to our children."

I was truly stunned as I tried to grasp the implications of his statement. If what he was saying was true, then I had been running ahead of my husband. All the stress and guilt I was feeling over my failure to live up to super-missionary status were mine and mine alone. Ellie felt no such guilt because he felt no such inappropriate ambition. His only ambition could be summed up in one word: 'Faithfulness.' And if that was the only ambition that Ellie was concerned about, then I, as his wife, could relax.

At that moment it was as if a huge burden was instantly lifted off my shoulders. I was free from trying to be a *Practically*

Perfect Pedestal Person! I already knew that I had failed to be one, but now I realized that I wasn't even *supposed* to be one. I was just supposed to follow my husband, however he led.

"So does this mean," I tentatively asked, "that we don't *have* to be missionaries in Guatemala, or anywhere else?"

"Of course we don't!" was Ellie's reply. "We *can* be missionaries if we want to, but we can also do something else instead if we like."

"You mean, you could become a plumber or a carpenter if you wanted to, and that would be okay?" I asked.

"Of course!" he replied emphatically.

Now, at this point in my story, you may be tempted to think, "Gosh she's cute, but she's not too bright!" You may be wondering why this concept was so difficult for me to grasp. Well, you have to realize that for as long as I could remember, I had not only had a desire to be a missionary, but also a sense of *obligation* to be one. Several of my aunts and uncles and cousins were missionaries—you might say it was our family business. All of my friends and family expected me to be one, because of course I had been announcing that intention since I was eleven years old. So for me to suddenly be free to 'switch horses mid-stream' if I so desired...well, it was mind-boggling! It was also totally liberating! From that point on, my whole perspective on missionary service came into sharper focus.

I don't want to give the impression, however, that it was through counseling and counseling alone that God brought such freedom and healing to my life. Counseling played a big part, but the other wonderful thing happening at the same time was that God was ministering a new work of the Holy Spirit to me through several different sources.

I was attending a non-denominational ladies' Bible study with my sister, Shannie, and at the end of each session the ladies would lay hands on and pray for anyone who needed prayer. Their prayers really ministered to my broken spirit.

Another time, Ev Schroeder, a pastor's wife whom I had just met, asked me if she could share 'a word from the Lord' with me. I wasn't familiar with that terminology, but I said, "Sure, go ahead."

Ev described the following: "I saw you and your family in the eye of a tornado. It was dark and noisy and things were violently swirling around you, but you were kept safe because you were all being held in God's hand. After a while, God gently lowered you to the ground through the middle of all the turmoil, and the tornado ceased, and the sun came out."

That was it. That was all she said, and she didn't really know what it meant. But I did. To me it was such an accurate picture of what we had been going through and such a blessed promise for the future. It gave me hope.

Perhaps the most significant ministry of the Holy Spirit to my hurting soul came through our new friends Ed and Olly Alexander. When we arrived from Guatemala, bruised and bleeding, so to speak, they literally took us into their home and made us part of their family. They invested hours and hours opening Scripture to us, encouraging us and praying over us. God used them in a mighty way to bring me true healing, and a newfound joy and power in the Holy Spirit.

As we searched for new direction, Ellie said that the most important thing now was to allow Caleb to heal. Therefore, in whatever we decided to do, establishing a secure home had to be a priority. Other than that, he said, we were free to consider any options.

Over the next few weeks we prayed and explored various possibilities of what we might like to do. None of the options really grabbed us until we got a letter from our friend, John Jessup. He had also been in Guatemala and had recently returned to his home in the Hood River Valley of Oregon. John was deeply impressed by the spiritual needs of the Mexican migrant workers there, and was concerned that there was no

Spanish-speaking Christian church in the valley. He suggested that we might consider going to live and minister there.

That letter was a catalyst in our thinking. God seemed to speak to our hearts saying, "Yes, this is right. This is what I want you to do. Go ahead." The great thing about it was that there we were, considering another full-time ministry, but this time *not* out of a sense of duty and obligation. Instead, it was with joy and anticipation that we looked forward to a new chapter in our lives.

Post-Pedestal Pondering

Although God does not allow His servants to persist in sinful pride, His efforts to humble us are always in love and mercy. His intent is not to destroy, but to restore. Unlike Humpty Dumpty, God's servants *can* be put back together again after suffering a great fall. All the King's horses and all the King's men cannot accomplish healing on their own, but the King does use His people to touch the lives of His broken servants.

During those previous slow months of healing back in British Columbia, God taught me that it's okay for full-time Christian workers to:

- Admit that they need help

- Get counseling

- Ask for prayer

- Question their motives

- Examine their true identity

- Relinquish inappropriate ambitions

God is not threatened or surprised by the weaknesses of His children. He knows us intimately and can handle any reconstruction job, no matter how big! If you are trying to minister while laboring under guilt, inappropriate ambition, or overwhelming failure, it may be time to get help. Admit your brokenness, and let the King put you back together again!

CHAPTER FIVE

Inching Along Towards Maturity...with the Help of My Kids

From the lips of children and infants you have
ordained praise...
Psalm. 8:2

Pride, insecurity, ungodly ambition, a false sense of obligation, people-pleasing tendencies—I hope you can see that the sins and weaknesses that I struggled with as a rookie missionary were the same ones that anyone might struggle with. Vocational Christian workers are not exempt from such destructive patterns, but nor do we have a corner of the market on them. These problems are common to the human race in general.

I'd like to say that by the time we began our new ministry in Oregon I was fully cured of all of the above shortcomings. I'd *like* to say that, but then I would have to add 'liar' to an already too long list of my character flaws. Nope...best to tell the truth. The truth is, although I had recently taken a quantum leap forward, I still had a lot of growing up to do.

It was the summer of 1989 when we set out to start a Spanish-speaking church among the Mexican migrant workers of the Hood River Valley. At the time we had no idea what a huge undertaking that would be. I could write a whole book just on our triumphs and failures in that endeavor alone. But that book will have to wait, because this chapter is dedicated to my children.

Caleb had just turned four when we moved to Oregon. As we established order and stability in our home, it was wonderful to see his physical symptoms begin to subside. His hair grew back in, and as long as he stayed in a predictable routine, his skin stayed relatively clear. For years, however, any time we would travel to visit our churches in British Columbia for a week, or even go away for a weekend, Caleb's rash would return with a vengeance. His little body simply couldn't handle the stress.

As his health began to improve, however, another almost more serious problem began to emerge. Caleb was very bright and very strong-willed. Being the eldest child, he had become used to thinking that he was the center of the universe. For a year, we had been so consumed by his health problems that we had neglected to train or discipline him properly. It started to become obvious that we had created a monster.

We resolved to do everything in our power to save this kid. We had left the mission field in Guatemala largely to save his life. Now that we were aware of this other problem, we weren't about to sacrifice him on the altar of over-indulgence. But believe me, there was no instant cure for this 'disease,' either. Just as it had taken four years to create a monster, so it took at *least* the next four years to undo the damage.

I remember walking around all those years constantly carrying a wooden spoon in the back pocket of my jeans, ready to whip it out should the situation demand it. The trouble was that the situation demanded it so very frequently! Each night I would fall into bed exhausted from the battle of wills that this child would put me through. I knew that he was stronger than I was, but I wasn't about to let *him* know that. Sometimes I despaired of ever coming out on top, but Ellie assured me that we were making progress, slow though it seemed. And as we cried out to God for help, God was faithful to answer.

Now that Caleb is grown, people can hardly believe it when I describe what a terrible kid we had allowed him to become, and what a struggle it was to correct it. Today he's a godly, responsible young man who loves the Lord and unselfishly serves others with his gifts and talents.

At least a decade after my showdown with Caleb, a friend lent me a book called *To Train Up a Child*, by Michael and Debi Pearl. If I had known then the principles of child training that the Pearls explain in their book, I could have saved myself countless hassles with Caleb. Even so, the book has been a real help in training subsequent children. I re-read it often.

We started homeschooling the year that Caleb was four and Josh was two. Although, as you already know, I am one of the most arts- and crafts-challenged people on this planet, I had fun learning to do *very simple* craft projects with the boys. It was gratifying to see how pleased they were just to glue the cotton balls onto the picture of the sheep. I could handle a craft like that!

It was also fun over the next couple of years working with math manipulatives, going on nature hikes, and putting memory verses to music. We joined a homeschool co-op, and that was fun, too. But when I started to teach Josh how to read, I ceased to have fun.

Josh was four at the time, and since Caleb had basically taught himself to read when he was four, I assumed that four was the correct age to begin teaching phonics. Accordingly,

I began to put Josh through his paces, only to meet with utter bewilderment on his part. "What on earth is she *talking* about?" he must have wondered.

What I didn't recognize was that Josh is about as different from Caleb as two brothers can be. Whereas Caleb is intense and cerebral, Josh is friendly and easygoing. Whereas Caleb is driven and self-motivated, Josh is relaxed and non-competitive. I failed to take these personality differences into account when I tried to teach Josh to read, and since he failed to 'get it,' I could only assume that I was doing something wrong.

So I switched tactics. I tried another reading program. Then another. And another. Finally I decided that he must be a bit too young, so I should try again the following year. Which I did. And the year after that. And the year after that. All in all, it took five years and four different programs to teach Josh to read. I never did hit upon the 'right' program... I merely decided to go back to the original one that I had started with, but *this* time to persevere. And one day, when Josh was nine, I woke up suddenly to the realization that he could read just fine, and he even enjoyed it!

In retrospect, I should never have attempted to teach a four-year-old child to read, unless he wanted to learn and had sufficient pre-reading skills. But I didn't know that at the time. Also, running into the kind of learning roadblocks that I ran into with Josh, I should have suspected and tested for dyslexia. But I didn't know that either.

Josh was a guinea pig for this inexperienced home-schooling teacher. Though he got frustrated and tearful at times, he was mostly cheerful while his frantic mother experimented with program after program. Josh and I learned patience and perseverance together through the whole ordeal. I sometimes marvel that he wasn't scarred for life by his terrible experience with a pushy mother. But the grace of God clearly moved in to cover my mistakes. Today Josh is a handsome, athletic young man who loves extreme sports. He is strong, not just in body, but also in character and in his love for God and others.

Lucas, our irrepressible third-born, teaches me that life is fun and that every task is a new opportunity to enjoy oneself. He also taught me never to turn my back on a toddler—not even for a moment. While I was doing lessons at the kitchen table with Caleb and Josh, Lucas (two years old at the time) would be out the front door and down the street. Total strangers would bring him home asking if this was our child. I experimented with every trick in the parenting book to try to keep him home. Once I even tied him to the piano so I could go to the bathroom. The little Houdini was gone when I came out! Finally Ellie installed a deadbolt high up on our door where Lucas couldn't reach it. He also built a fence. By the time Lucas turned three, I was a nervous wreck, but I had certainly improved in the Attentive Mother category.

Isaac motivated me to get organized. When we had just three children, I could sort of muddle along in my own haphazard fashion, and the laundry would eventually get done. Isaac's birth changed all that. Now I was overwhelmed with nursing a newborn, chasing a two-year-old, home-schooling the two older boys, and participating in a very challenging church-planting ministry. I needed a system! A Mormon friend of mine who had seven children showed me her day-planner system, and I was hooked. I could not have survived all these incredibly busy years with a growing family without an organizational plan.

Isaac's inquiring mind inspires me to search out the reasons *why*. His artistic nature prompts me to see the beauty in God's world. And his gentle, sensitive spirit reminds me to slow down and to listen. Isaac's drive to create is something that I don't understand, but I do admire.

After having four boys in a row, I was convinced that I would just continue to have boys. So I was completely shocked the moment Johanna was born and Ellie exclaimed, "Lila, it's a girl!" Almost my first thought was, "But I don't know how to fix girls' hair!" That was eight years ago, and I *still* haven't learned to do French braids. But Johanna teaches me so many other things. She is a little lady—not a tomboy like I was. Through her, I learn to delight in flowers and frills, tea parties and dolls, soft music and a beautifully set table. Johanna is my reminder to weave the feminine graces throughout our male-dominated home. She is also naturally organized, helping me to anticipate and prepare for events ahead of time, instead of just winging it as I go—my natural procrastinating tendency.

Benjamin is six now, and he's good at it. His self-confidence is inspiring to me, as he analyzes each new situation and comes up with his own explanations for the whys and wherefores. As the saying goes, "He may be wrong, but he's never in doubt!" Benjy's tears of joy when he gave his life to Jesus remind me to be grateful for my salvation. And his tender concern for his mother touches my heart.

Esther is our three-year-old delight. She is such a charmer that I am constantly reminded of the need to emphasize *character* development, not external beauty. Her trust of animals and even total strangers makes me wonder whether I trust my Lord Jesus as much—He who has proven Himself trustworthy throughout all eternity. Esther is a gift from God.

The unborn baby that I am carrying is an unknown entity at this point, but has already proven to be a blessing. The severe nausea that I experience in the first trimester with each pregnancy forces me to cry out to God. When I feel so sick that I want to die, He sustains me and somehow gets me through. It is always a blessing to throw myself on God's mercy and to find that He is faithful. This baby has forced me to do that again and again, and for that I am thankful.

Strangers in the grocery store often say things to me like, "Oh, I could never have four children" (or five or six or whatever number I happened to have at the time). "I could never homeschool my kids... I'm too disorganized and impatient," they continue. My standard reply is that so am I! It seems, though, that as God blesses us with more children, He also increases my organizational skills (which were nil to start with). It is also through my children that I learn patience and so many other needed character qualities. As the old song goes, "He giveth more grace when the burdens grow greater; He sendeth more strength when the labors increase."

Children are a blessing...that's a fact. We used to sing in Sunday school, "God said it! I believe it! That settles it!" But *do* you really believe it? If you have children, are they a blessing or a handicap to your current ministry? We went through a period of time when our children were a handicap to ours.

I remember the day after our fourth son was born, my father-in-law told me, "Okay Lila, now it's time to stop. You and Ellie shouldn't have any more kids." I asked him why not and he replied "God has called you to minister, and your kids are getting in the way." I was angry, hurt, and chagrined...because I knew that he spoke the truth. Our children were *not* a blessing to our ministry at that time. They were whiny, disruptive, and disobedient. Our family was a poor example to the newly converted Hispanic parents whom we were trying to disciple.

My father-in-law's criticism was a wake-up call to me. If Ellie and I could not bring our children into line, then we had no business being in pastoral ministry. That is one of the biblical requirements of leadership (1 Timothy 3:4,5).

Ellie and I faced up to our negligence in child-training, and with God's help we slowly began to make the needed changes in the discipline of our children. We also began to train our children to take responsibility in the work of the church, and to view this whole endeavor as our *family* ministry—not just Dad and Mum's thing. The boys set up chairs for our services, passed out songbooks, and helped decorate for parties. As they grew older, they did special music, collected the offering, and helped teach Sunday school. Our children struggled and prayed alongside us as we shared in ministry together.

But I must be clear here. There was no substitute for the proper discipline of our children. Handing out hymnbooks could not cure rebellious hearts. Disobedience and rebellion needed to be firmly addressed before our small children could bring us great joy. However, as they were gradually brought under control, then our place of ministry was an ideal training ground for them to begin to develop the needed character qualities of compassion, responsibility, and patience.

We realized that because God has given us these specific children, then they are to be our *main* ministry. Any pastoral or missions responsibilities are to be our *general* assignment, but our children are assigned to us by name. If they are proving to be a bane rather than a blessing in our life and work, then it is time to make some changes. Ellie and I need to listen constantly to the message that God is sending through our kids. If they are acting out and causing problems, then it is obvious that they need more attention/love/discipline/training/time than we are giving them. The other possibility is that they might need a change of environment or relief from peer pressure that they may be experiencing. This was one of the factors that motivated us to consider homeschooling.

We will never regret any sacrifice necessary to help our children walk with God, including leaving the mission field for a season. However, I would bitterly regret it if I were to place a high priority on ushering *others* into the Kingdom while my own children fall by the wayside.

In terms of sheer productivity, devoting myself to raising two or three children (or seven or eight!) did not always appear to be the most effective use of my time. Small children have little to recommend them but their charms; however, God in His wisdom has deemed that, for a season, their charms are enough. My hope and prayer as they grow – and they grow oh so quickly! – is that all of my children will become increasingly more productive in God's kingdom, giving multiple returns on my initial time investment.

Since the apple never falls far from the tree, my children are a far cry from perfection. Some have hair issues, some have self-control issues, some have bossiness issues – every one of them is very human. Nevertheless, God is pleased to use them and to reveal Himself in their weaknesses. While the younger ones are busy making inroads into peoples' hearts through their sweet smiles and hugs, the older ones can now help in many different areas of service: leading worship, constructing an orphanage, hosting mission work teams, sharing hospitality, promoting missions through musical concerts...the list goes on and on. Through their combined efforts, my children can touch more lives with the love of God than I could ever hope to reach in my lifetime.

Post-Pedestal Pondering

I firmly believe that each child that God sends is intended to be a blessing, not just to the world, but also to his or her parents. Children are not given just to be cute or to gratify our egos. They are given to help develop character in us, their parents, whether we parents realize it or not. Each one of my children has taught me innumerable lessons, developed a little more Christ-likeness in me, and nudged me a little further along the path to maturity.

Ask God to give you a vision of the Kingdom purposes that He wants to accomplish through your family, and then invest whatever effort is necessary to make it happen.

Remember that your children:

- Are given to be a blessing

- Need to be trained and disciplined

- Can disqualify you from ministry if neglected

- Should be your Number One ministry

- Will help you develop godly character

You have such a small window of opportunity to train your precious children in God's ways...don't miss your chance!

Pop Quiz Number One

Question:
The main point of this book so far is that: (choose one)

a. Pastors and missionaries are not the sharpest tools in the shed.

b. Anyone aspiring to vocational Christian service should have his or her head examined.

c. Missionaries are miserable people.

d. Full-time Christian workers are the same as other people, suffer the same as other people, and have the same tough lessons to learn as other people.

If you chose (a), (b), or (c), then it is obvious that I need to go back and rewrite the first few chapters. If you chose (d), congratulations…you are right! You have correctly discerned the sometimes veiled intent of all my ramblings.

To review: God chooses ordinary Christians to serve Him full-time; however, sometimes ordinary Christians have pride/insecurity/codependency issues to work through. God is more concerned about developing Christ-likeness in His servants than He is about His people achieving 'maximum productivity.' In His great love and mercy, He will use the pressures and trials of ministry to help His loved ones mature in Christ. He will also teach them enduring lessons of His faithfulness through the lives of their own children.

Are you with me so far? If you failed the quiz, please take it over again until you can pass, and then proceed to the next chapter.

CHAPTER SIX

My Worst Nightmare— the Death of a Child

Weeping may remain for a night, but rejoicing comes in the morning.
Psalm 30:5b

We had been living in the Hood River Valley for ten years, and life was good. Ellie was fulfilled and happy in his ministry to the Hispanic community, and I helped out where I could: teaching a Bible study to Mexican ladies, extending hospitality, and organizing potlucks and other church functions. We lived in a little old farmhouse on one and a half acres with our six beautiful children. The kids had lots of room to run, raise goats, chickens, and steers, and to learn a strong work ethic. My days were full with Little League baseball games, gardening (though I did a pathetic job of it), canning, cooking, kids' music lessons, and homeschooling. As I say, life was good. And that was my problem.

Deep down I suspected that things were *too* good, and that any moment the axe was going to fall. My recurring nightmare was that God would take one of my children — and I knew that I could never survive such a loss. I had not yet learned to trust the heart of God.

My fear was such that if any of my children were going somewhere, I would sometimes stand at the window and cry, sure that I would never see them again. Even if Ellie was only taking the kids to Grandma's house for the day, I pictured a child drowning in the pond, or falling from a tree. When someone was late arriving home, I would mentally start planning their funeral. The mother's love that I felt for my children was deep, but it was also possessive. In my heart, I was desperately clinging to my children as if they were my own possessions — not gifts on loan to us from God.

It was the summer of 1998 on the last evening of our family vacation at the Cannon Beach Conference Center. After the evening service, we asked the guest speaker to pray for us and for some of the ministry challenges that we were facing. As he finished praying for our ministry, he threw in something extra along these lines: "Lord, I also pray for this new little life that my sister here is carrying. Bless this child, and fulfill all Your good purposes for this child's life. Amen."

We thanked the pastor and walked back to our room, and I was just mortified. *Am I really that fat, that he thinks I'm pregnant? I thought I was looking pretty good, but I guess a whole week of this wonderful Cannon Beach food has done a number on me. Now I'm looking pregnant again! Man, I'm starting on a diet the minute we get home!* That was my spiritual response to a godly man's prophetic prayer.

As it turned out, a couple of weeks later I found out that I was indeed pregnant with our seventh child. The pregnancy went along smoothly — that is, as smoothly as it ever goes for me: horrible nausea in the first trimester, followed by relative energy and a sense of well-being in the second trimester.

It wasn't until the third trimester that I had an inkling that something might be wrong.

At a routine prenatal checkup, my midwives asked me how I was doing. Suddenly I burst into tears blubbering out: "I'm so fat, and this baby is so heavy to carry, and I'm only seven months along and as big as a house, and how can I possibly carry this baby full term!" You may be thinking, "Oh yeah, typical. Pregnancy hormones, wacko emotions. Every mother thinks she's huge." Of course I know that's true, but I really *was* huge! Even taking into account that my babies average between ten and eleven pounds at birth, with the most recent one weighing eleven pounds, two ounces, I was still measuring big for seven months. I looked like I was due any minute, and I was *so* tired.

My sweet midwives sympathized and prayed with me, and then explained: "Lila, you have polyhydramnios—excess amniotic fluid. You are carrying so much extra liquid that it is difficult for us to palpate the baby. It's a bit of a red flag because sometimes polyhydramnios can indicate a problem with the baby." They suggested that we have an ultrasound done to put our minds at rest.

Obediently, Ellie and I went to see our local Christian family doctors. Apparently they detected something a little odd on the screen, because they recommended that we go into Portland and get a second opinion from a specialist. So we made an appointment for the following week—the soonest we could get in.

It was during that week of waiting that I had the dream. One morning when I woke up, my pillow was soaked with tears. I had been dreaming that instead of the lovely, quiet home births that I was used to, that this baby's birth turned into a nightmare of medical intervention. In my dream, I was transported to the hospital, had all sorts of complications requiring all sorts of treatment, and in the end my baby died. It was an absolute worst case scenario that my subconscious mind was playing out.

When I told my friend, Pam, about my dream, she lovingly tried to reassure me that of course that wasn't going to happen. "Stop fearing the worst, and trust God," she told me. But as I explained to Pam, in a way the dream had actually helped me. "It was like facing up to all the horrifying possibilities and looking them in the eye. Somehow it helped me to confront my fears."

The day of my appointment came, and Ellie and I made the one and a half-hour trip to downtown Portland. "Yes, there is something amiss," the doctor said, "but I can't tell what." He sent me to St. Vincent's Hospital to have yet *another* ultrasound done on even more specialized equipment.

As Ellie and I dutifully traipsed from doctor to doctor, we didn't feel any panic. Although we realized that there could be something seriously wrong, we have a fairly healthy dose of skepticism towards gloom-and-doom doctors who always predict the worst. Maybe we've heard too many stories of doctors recommending an abortion based on an ultrasound result, only later to discover that the baby is perfect after all!

At any rate, we were calm when the St. Vincent's doctor told us solemnly that there was something seriously wrong with our child. "The baby will need an operation the minute it is born," he said, "You will have to stay here in Portland from now until the baby is born in order to be close to the specialized neo-natal unit at Emmanuel Hospital. You must not go home."

We sat in silence trying to absorb all of the doctor's recommendations, but it was the part about not going home that really threw me. *How can we not go home? We left our six kids with a babysitter thinking that I would just be gone for the day. How can I possibly stay in Portland for the next two months till my due date?*

Nevertheless, the doctor insisted that we lived too far away to risk going home, so Ellie and I said that we needed to talk about it and that we'd come back in a couple of hours.

We went downstairs to have lunch in the hospital cafeteria and to talk and pray.

As we were finishing our lunch, suddenly I went into labor! There was no mistaking the symptoms—this was my seventh child, after all—so we headed back upstairs in the elevator. Sure enough, I was in labor, and this was *way* too early. I needed to get over to Emmanuel Hospital STAT!

Ellie loaded me into the back of the van and drove like a maniac across the city to the other hospital. If ever there was a time to pray, it was then! But something surprising happened. As I was lying there, I felt the presence of God with me, and I sensed Him saying, "Lila, *don't* pray. Ellie can pray, and others can pray, but don't you pray. You give me *praise* and just rest."

It was amazing to think that I was being told *not* to do what I had always believed is the main task of every Christian. But my spirit immediately recognized why God might direct me this way. All through this pregnancy, I had prayed for this baby, and as the suspected problems arose, I pleaded with God for the baby to be born strong and healthy. I knew that, other than giving thanks, if I prayed at all in this situation, it would just deteriorate to begging and pleading for my baby's life. God was saying that He already knew my heart, He had heard my prayers, and He had it all under control. I could rest.

And rest I did. Throughout the next several days as the nightmare of medical intervention played itself out, I rested in the Lord. It was a deep peace that I felt—not one that I could manufacture by myself. It was a gift from God to carry me through the deep waters that were to come.

In spite of the doctors' heroic efforts to stop my labor, our beautiful baby girl was born three days later. She weighed four and a half pounds and was perfect in every visible way—except that she had a diaphragmatic hernia. Basically that means that she had a hole in her diaphragm that the intestines had pushed their way up through, taking up the space in her chest cavity where her lungs should have been developing. The doctors hoped that she would stabilize enough within the first twenty-four hours to allow them to operate, but she never did. After living for only fourteen hours, Naomi Joy went home to heaven.

I remember standing in the intensive care neo-natal unit watching Naomi die. My sister-in-law had lent me a lovely music tape called *Hope* by Sheila Walsh. It was playing on the portable stereo when I was just grasping the fact that my baby really was going to die. The words of the song at the moment were:

> *"And now I am standing with my face to the Son,*
> *and these are the best days of my life."*

I raised my eyes to the window, which showed only a gray, cloudy day outside, and at that moment God enveloped me in His love and comfort. The presence of the Son was so very real and so sweet at that moment that it truly did feel like one of the best days of my life.

And yet it was the very worst. The nightmare came true. My baby died. And there was nothing I could do to bring her back. The pain was excruciating. All I could do was wade in and let the waves of my grief crash over me. There was no way to avoid it, and no way to go through it quickly.

We took Naomi's little body home with us that night so that the children could see their baby sister. But the next morning I had to surrender her into the arms of the funeral home attendant, which just about killed me. How could I give up my baby?

Looking back on the days and weeks after Naomi's death, each moment seems drenched in sorrow. Giving her a bath at the funeral home, placing her in her little coffin, closing the lid, walking away—each task was beyond my ability to carry out. My grief was overwhelming. And yet, alongside the sorrow and in the midst of the grief, there ran a deep underlying current of joy. God met me there in my suffering, and His love comforted me. His gentle presence never left me even while the bitter tears seemed to never cease.

In the months that followed, as I sought and found comfort in God's Word, I came to really believe, maybe for the first time, that God's heart towards me truly is a heart of love. His plans for me are good plans, and when He allows tragedy to strike, it is for the purpose of pouring out a greater measure of His presence and His comfort.

Naomi's short life changed me in a way that I could never have anticipated. As my worst nightmare came true—the death of a child—it served to take away my fear of losing a child. I no longer stand crying at the window when my children leave for a period of time. I know now that they *could* die—after all, they are only on loan to us, and really belong to God. But I also know that if God has a purpose in calling them home, then He will give me the grace to survive my loss. And I know now that I can trust Him.

Post-Pedestal Pondering

I wish that entering full-time ministry would include a money-back guarantee of a painless, rosy life. Wouldn't that be a great recruitment pitch for mission agencies and under-staffed churches? "Come on board with us, and you will enjoy personal peace and affluence, good health, and a sorrow-free existence!" They'd be swamped with applicants.

But Jesus promised His servants just the opposite. He promised danger and persecution and the whole world against us. On the surface, it doesn't sound like much of a deal, but that's only part of it. He also promises to walk with us through all of life's challenges. When He allows the arrows of pain and sorrow to penetrate our hearts, He also gives His soothing presence. And we find that His presence is enough. Our God can be trusted to do what is best for us—always. His heart toward us is a heart of love. I know that now.

In Scripture we find that God's servants are guaranteed:

- Suffering and sorrow

- Comfort in the midst of pain

- God's presence in all of life's challenges

- Peace that passes all understanding

- Joy in the morning

Whether you have yet to walk through the deep waters of sorrow, have walked through them in the past, or are walking through them now, it is essential to remember that God's heart towards you *is* a heart of love—really and truly! He does not allow pain to touch your life on a mere capricious whim. When pain comes, remember that it is expertly designed to accomplish God's *good* purposes in your life. You can trust Him.

CHAPTER SEVEN

The Struggle for Jurisdiction

Do not set your mind on high things…
do not be wise in your own opinion.
Romans 12:16 (NKJV)

The little town of Parkdale, in the Hood River Valley of Oregon, is an idyllic setting. Situated at the base of majestic Mt. Hood, nestled among the apple and pear orchards, with friendly farmers and retro values—it truly contains the best of both worlds. Not only is it small-town apple-pie Americana at its finest, but it also holds a little slice of Mexican hot tamale pie. The migrant workers who live and work there lend a special cross-cultural flavor to life in the Hood River Valley. It couldn't have been a better place for us to live and minister.

Given such a perfect environment, things should have been perfect. But the trouble with all Christian workers (including me) is that we are imperfect people. And even people who love the Lord Jesus and are committed to serving Him struggle at times with sin. My besetting sin during those pastoral ministry years was that of trying to control my husband. Perhaps this confession will shock and disgust some of you; nevertheless, it is true. I was guilty (and frequently continue to be guilty) of the same heinous crime that Eve committed in the Garden.

Apart from my natural proclivity as a daughter of Eve to fall into the same trap she did, I think that there was another major contributing factor. My whole underlying philosophy of our ministry had a fatal flaw, which skewed the entire church-planting endeavor from day one. In my mind, Ellie and I were equal partners in pastoral ministry. I believed that God had called both of us to pastor a church among the Hispanic community. It was to be a joint venture. Of course, Ellie would be the *real* pastor, but I would be working behind the scenes to give him direction and inspiration. It never occurred to me that this is the exact job description of a puppet master controlling a puppet on a string.

Naturally, Ellie himself did not adhere to this same philosophy. If he had known what seeds had planted themselves in my mind, I'm sure he would have attempted to uproot them. But he didn't know. Like the myth of *Practically Perfect Pedestal People* in chapter two, I held this belief at a subconscious level.

Before you denounce me as a female chauvinist pig bent on restricting women to subservient roles, please hear me out. I am not saying here that women cannot be equal partners in ministry (or business or whatever) with their husbands. What I am saying is that *I* was not to be an equal partner. It was not the right season in my life to be overly involved in anything except 'wife-ing' and 'mothering.'

We had willingly chosen to let God plan our family size and spacing, and we were joyfully homeschooling our growing brood of children out of conviction. My hands were full—more than full! With Ellie's blessing, I was a stay-at-home mum trying to nurture and train and raise our kids to be mighty in God's Kingdom. With so much on my plate, what business did I have thinking that I could be an equal partner with an equal interest in the church-planting enterprise? None! But I did think that, and it took years of frustration before God proved me wrong.

Oh, it started out innocently enough. In those early years of our ministry in the Valley, Ellie and I would sit and brainstorm over strategies for reaching the Hispanic population with the Gospel. We would pray about a plan of action, and then Ellie would ask me to take part in implementing it. For example, knowing that the way to men's hearts is through their stomachs, we would decide to have a potluck after each Bible study or church service. Fine. I could organize it and cook for it—no problem. In that case I was complying with what Ellie asked me to do. I was his 'help-meet' as per Genesis chapter two.

As another example, it soon became all too obvious that the unchurched Mexican kids who were coming to our services were largely undisciplined and unable to sit quietly for any length of time in a service. We had little kids running up and down the aisles, jumping off of chairs, and yelling at their hapless parents during our worship services! Something had to be done...and quickly.

Ellie asked me to start a children's church class, which I was only too happy to do since I was having a major struggle trying to control our own kids during the service. For several years after that, I taught all ages together, usually with a nursing baby attached, and my own kids doing their best to be as disruptive as possible. (Remember, it took years to whip Caleb into shape, and Josh and Lucas were coming up through the ranks emulating their bratty older brother!) So it was certainly not an ideal situation, but there was no one else to help, and I was doing what Ellie wanted and needed me to do at the time. (God, in His mercy, eventually sent along wonderful, godly families to take over the children's ministry... but that's another story.)

I was also responsible for writing prayer letters to our supporting churches and friends, and for keeping up with the church bookkeeping, with the faithful help of a dear friend. After a few years, Ellie asked me to start up a ladies' Bible study in Spanish, which I thoroughly enjoyed. So you see that it was certainly not a case of my pining away for lack of a significant ministry to be involved in. I had ministry coming out of my ears—as much as I could handle and far more besides! What more could I possibly want? Only this: control.

It irked me when Ellie didn't do things the way I thought they should be done. It bothered me when he spent his time on ministry projects that I didn't think were the highest priority. I would get very annoyed when he neglected to ask for my opinion on important church-related issues, or when he deliberately did things contrary to what I thought was best. *Why does he have to be so stubborn? Why doesn't he listen to me? Why can't a man be more like a woman?*

It really irritated me when he didn't use enough illustrations in his sermons, so I set out to remedy that. I started a little file of sermon illustrations for him, and every week I would ask him for the topic of his upcoming sermon. Then I would search the file and find catchy illustrations for him to use. I laid them all out on his desk and sometimes even penciled them in at appropriate places throughout the text of his sermon. I was being terribly helpful, I thought, just like a church secretary.

There was one small problem, though. Ellie had not asked me to help in this area, and in fact he usually didn't *want* my help. But of course I insisted, and the result was a lot of tension between us. Many times he didn't even use the illustrations that I had so carefully picked out and that were obviously so perfect for the text. That's when I would see red! *How dare he make his own decisions about how he wants to preach, and ignore all the hard work that I do for him? I thought we were supposed to be equal partners in this thing, and so he should cooperate when I tell him what to do!*

Our struggle, you see, was over jurisdiction. Who was the real authority in this ministry? Who had the final say? Was I a major stockholder with fifty-one per cent of the shares and the controlling vote, or was I just an employee, so to speak? As pastor of the fledgling church, was Ellie obligated to take my wishes into account since I was his helper and contributed some of the ideas? Was I within my rights to get upset when he set aside my plans and substituted others? Who was the boss here anyway? The answers to those questions had huge implications, not only for the ministry but also for our marriage.

Now obviously the head of the Church is Christ. He is The Boss. I understood that. But when it came down to the nitty-gritty of day-to-day operations, whose decisions were to carry the most weight? I was having such a hard time because I wanted to control Ellie and make him dance to *my* song. Everything went along just fine as long as Ellie would cooperate. But Ellie got his marching orders from Someone other than me, and those orders did not always correspond to what I thought was best. The truth was that I had no jurisdiction over Ellie.

Can you see the tightrope that God was asking me to walk? I was supposed to be Ellie's 'help-meet' — going out of my way to assist him in the areas where he requested and needed my help. Yet I was not supposed to allow my involvement to become a control issue. Being a helper did not confer authority upon me over Ellie or over the church. Being a helper meant that I was to be…a *helper*. Not a manager. Since I had such vested interests in seeing our ministry succeed, I found it very difficult to walk the fine line between offering assistance and manipulating results.

Over the years I frequently lost my balance and fell off the tightrope, insisting that assistance implied authority. God used the bumps and bruises both in our marriage and in the church to gradually teach me some lessons. He taught me the beauty of graciously offering help, and graciously deferring if the help is turned down. He taught me to allow my husband to make decisions affecting the family and the church, whether or not those decisions meet with my approval. God taught me to trust Him to work even through my husband's mistakes, leaving the results with Him.

I could have avoided years of low- to medium-grade conflict had I learned some of these lessons earlier. Unfortunately, I am basically stubborn and strong-willed, so it takes a long time to drive anything through my thick skull. I still struggle (often!) with the same ungodly tendencies to manipulate and control my husband. Maybe the only difference between now and those earlier years is that now, at least, I recognize those strivings as sin.

Post-Pedestal Pondering

To state the obvious, no one in ministry is exempt from sin. Each career Christian worker has his or her own battles with temptation, but I suspect that wives of pastors and missionaries are particularly susceptible to:

- Trying to manipulate and control their husbands

- Being critical of their husbands' priorities

- Failing to support and encourage their husbands' Kingdom efforts

- Becoming irritated if their suggestions and insights are neglected

- Not trusting God to work through their husbands.

From my experience, perhaps you will notice that entering vocational Christian service does not automatically thrust one onto a higher spiritual level. Sometimes, as was the case with me, it accomplishes quite the opposite. The pressures and trials of ministry often create just the right conditions for many of our nasty little faults to come spilling out. It can be ugly, but it's actually a beneficial process. Like lancing a boil, God wants to cleanse us and remove the defiling pus before it contaminates everything in and around us.

Does this accurately describe your current situation? Are you striving for control in a ministry over which you have no jurisdiction? If so, then repent now. You will find no peace until you surrender your desire for control to the Lord. If you are undergoing some painful surgical procedures, don't resist the Master Surgeon's knife. He knows exactly what needs to be cut out to make you effective in His service.

CHAPTER EIGHT

Burn-Out!

You have said, 'It is futile to serve God.
What did we gain by carrying out his
requirements and going about like
mourners before the Lord Almighty?'
Malachi 3:14

For eleven years we thoroughly enjoyed our church-planting ministry among the Hispanic community of the Hood River Valley. Even though it could never be said that the church grew 'by leaps and bounds,' most of the time we could discern small, incremental steps of progress. However, since I am more results-oriented than Ellie, sometimes I would get discouraged with our small congregation and the slow growth rate. Ellie would remind me that true success is to be faithful in whatever God gives us to do. He was definitely God's man for the job in those pioneering years because he seldom succumbed to discouragement. Although at times the ministry was difficult, we were both mostly energized by the challenge and convinced that we were doing exactly what God wanted us to do.

Until the twelfth year. The year we both burned out.

Tasks that had previously seemed rewarding now seemed only to sap our energy. Evangelism and outreach tools that achieved amazing results elsewhere seemed to fall flat in our hands. A persistent cynicism crept into our thinking, replacing our characteristic optimism. We had a hard time seeing God's power working through us. Our prayers for our church didn't seem to penetrate the ceiling.

For the first time we talked seriously of giving up because we felt that we had nothing left to give. We were confused—torn between different possible strategies: (a) Work harder, do better, run faster; (b) Stop running, and pray more; or (c) Quit.

Depending on the moment, each strategy had its appeal. So we simply didn't know what to do. I'd like to be able to say that my eyes were completely focused on the Lord Jesus during that time, but my discouragement ran so deep that I felt betrayed by God. I prayed, and it seemed that God did not answer. We worked, and He did not seem to bless the work of our hands. I demanded to know when God was going to give us some real victories in our ministry, because, God knows, that particular year we were well familiar with the humiliation of defeat. I cried out to Him, but He remained silent.

Like the Israelites whom God rebuked in Malachi 3:13-14, I began to think that it was futile to serve God. *Why risk all, give all, bleed so much for these people, and pray so hard, if it is all for nothing? What do we gain?* I felt hurt and jerked around by God— whom I had loved for my whole life.

About that time, our district supervisor encouraged us to attend a church-planting seminar in Seattle for Hispanic pastors and their wives. We dutifully obeyed and went, but the results of that trip were far different than what our supervisor had anticipated.

On the way to Seattle, Ellie and I daydreamed about what we would like to do if we weren't committed to our little Spanish church. *What would we like for our kids to experience if we were free to change the plan?* We fantasized about volunteering on a short-term basis for different missions in Mexico and Guatemala. We imagined how wonderful it would be to pursue a different path—if only for a few months.

By the time we reached Seattle, we were thinking outside the box. We were no longer doggedly determined to endure a ministry that we had come to view as endlessly draining. Now we were exploring ways to possibly take a sabbatical or a leave of absence or even to resign outright. In fact, in Seattle we spent a lot of time working behind the scenes trying to interest unassigned Hispanic pastors in a potential ministry at our little church!

At any rate, after that weekend, we knew that our hearts were no longer committed to staying in Hood River. We met with our district supervisor and confessed our discouragement and inability to persevere in the pastoral ministry given our state of mind. We explained that we felt we had given all we had to give, and that we would be more of a liability than an asset if we continued. It was with a tremendous sense of relief that we received our supervisor's counsel and blessing and made plans to submit our resignation to the church.

Yet, it was still difficult to walk away from the tiny church that we had founded. For years we had poured our blood, sweat, and tears into birthing and nurturing this church. Now it was time for us to leave. We faced a major hurdle convincing our dear church friends that it was best for them if we left. After all, we had led many of them to Christ and discipled them in their new faith. How could we abandon them now? They didn't understand that we *had* to leave in order to make room for the new pastor that God would bring.

As our last Sunday approached, there were many tears. Still, we knew without a doubt that God was releasing us from a burden that had become too heavy for us to bear. So in January Ellie preached his last sermon, we hugged our friends, and we said goodbye to our beloved little church.

There was only one small problem. What were we supposed to do now? Without an ongoing ministry, we could not continue to receive ongoing funds from our supporters. How would we pay our bills and put food on the table? More importantly, what was it that *God* wanted us to do? Did He still have a useful role for His tired, worn-out servants to fill?

Post-Pedestal Pondering

As Christian workers, all of us face the challenge of discerning how God wants us to serve, where, and for how long. My grandfather served as the pastor of his church for forty-three years. Nowadays, a three or four year pastoral turnover is not uncommon. Is there a happy medium between these two extremes? Perhaps...but every situation is different. God may call a particular minister to serve the same church or mission field for twenty years, and someone else as an interim servant for only six months.

How can we discern when we are called to carry on in spite of all obstacles, or when our service in any given location is truly drawing to a close? Every person in ministry probably has a different opinion on that subject, and I do not pretend to have a definitive answer. However, I do believe that there are a few general principles that can be gleaned from our experience.

I need to emphasize that you should never make a decision to stay or leave a ministry based solely on:

- Numerical results

- Discouragement

- Financial/job security

Nor should success in any ministry be measured by visible results, or emotional fulfillment, but by:

- A conviction that you are doing what God has called you to do

- The counsel and blessing of those in authority over you

- Faithfulness in spite of setbacks

That's it! That's about all I have to offer on the subject of burn-out. Obviously this is not the authoritative work on the topic; however, if you are feeling completely unable to carry on in your ministry, I would encourage you first to dig deep in God's Word for direction. He is always faithful to guide His children when they look to Him. He may tell you, "Well done, good and faithful servant...carry on," or He may say, "Come with me by yourselves to a quiet place and get some rest."(Mark 6:31)

On the other hand, if depression is clinging so hard to your spirit that nothing seems able to shake it loose, then my uneducated guess is that it is time to seek help. You can't accomplish much when you are consistently working past the point of diminishing returns. It becomes a vicious cycle, because lack of productivity can lead to extreme job fatigue, which exacerbates the existing problem of depression. At that point, it is difficult to accurately interpret God's Word as it applies to you.

Ask the counsel of your supervisors. There is no shame in admitting your need for someone to help you discern God's will. Counselors exist to counsel. Advisers are longing to advise. Go ahead...make their day! Don't hide out in your damp little cave of despair. Allow God's trusted servants to help you expose your trouble to the light of His Word. The loving Shepherd will gently lead you on from there.

CHAPTER NINE

"Are You Nuts?!"

We are fools for Christ...
1 Corinthians 4:10a

After Ellie resigned the pastorate of our Spanish-speaking church, we faced some challenging decisions. If a change is as good as a rest, Ellie and I reasoned, then we didn't need to *leave* full-time ministry to restore our energy...we just needed to shift gears. In fact, we were not at all opposed to carrying on in some kind of ministry. We just recognized that we needed a break from the heavy responsibilities of leading and guiding a church.

This transition time in our lives might sound a bit scary and unsettling. The truth is, it was very exciting to be free to explore short-term opportunities with various missions. Our initial plan was to take one year to travel around Mexico and Guatemala helping out wherever we could.

Apparently that was not God's plan.

One evening we were sifting through the little pile of replies that we had received from the mission agencies we had contacted. As we talked and prayed about our options, an e-mail message arrived. It was from Jim and Jamie Loker, good friends of ours from the years we had spent in Guatemala. The letter was the equivalent of the newspaper printer's command to "Stop the presses!"

In essence it said, "Do not pass *Go*! Do not collect $200! Stop inquiring into other missions' needs! Do not even consider going anywhere else! *We* need you here in Oaxaca, Mexico! Come now!"

It was a compelling letter explaining potentially long-term ministry opportunities, which precisely matched our gifts and abilities. Ellie was thrilled at the prospect of helping Jim in Oaxaca, because God had already been laying the needs of Oaxaca on his heart, and nudging him in that direction. I, on the other hand, was a tiny bit annoyed with our friends for being so persuasive and swaying Ellie towards Oaxaca. I wanted to hold out for Mazatlan, Cancun, or Acapulco—any one of which was certainly more beautiful and exotic. *And besides, there is probably a tremendous evangelism need among all the tourists there on the beaches!*

This was a definite test of my previous commitment to learn to follow my husband's leading instead of scheming and manipulating to get my own way. I knew that God could and would lead Ellie in the right path, but I was also well aware of my proven ability as a wife to interfere with God's plan. *Do I really want to face the same kind of severe correction that I had received in Guatemala? Not on your life, baby!* So I kept my mouth shut.

As Ellie prayed, he became more and more convinced that God had opened the door to Oaxaca, and that we were supposed to walk through it. Given his conviction, eventually I, too, became enthusiastic at the prospect. Even our kids were eager to go south, learn Spanish, and 'get in touch with their Hispanic side.' They had always been slightly ashamed of the fact that being of half Mexican blood, they couldn't speak Spanish worth beans. Plus, they could tell that God seemed to be leading us in the direction of Oaxaca, and they wanted to be on board. Yes, they struggled with the idea of pulling up roots and leaving their friends, but ultimately they all wanted to obey God's voice. If He was saying, "Go," they were willing to go.

As we prayed about Oaxaca, we searched the Scriptures for confirmation. We consulted with our spiritual mentors and authorities in several churches. We talked to our parents and asked their advice. We also broached the idea to our financial supporters. Almost everyone across the board seemed to think that we should go for it. It was very reassuring to receive positive responses from almost everyone in our lives.

That's why we were unprepared for the reaction from some of our friends. In a nutshell, their response was, "Are you nuts?"

"You guys are crazy to consider hauling a family of seven kids thousands of miles away to a place you've never even seen before! It was bad enough that you traumatized Caleb with your previous missionary lifestyle—are you now planning to traumatize the other six? Kids need security—how can you think of uprooting them all from their happy lives in small-town America? Besides, you don't have the money to travel to Mexico, much less live there month after month and year after year!"

Most significantly, they thought we were being foolish to assume that God was guiding us when it appeared this was just something that *we* wanted to do. It seemed to them that we were presuming on God's faithfulness to sustain us while we ran ahead of His will. Our friends were alarmed that we, their previously sensible friends, had suddenly taken leave of our senses.

How could we answer their concerns? They were right on almost all accounts. It did seem crazy! Even though we had a deep sense of God calling us to Oaxaca, how could we explain or prove such a subjective feeling? We knew that we were hearing the voice of God, but how could we convince *them* of that? We couldn't. In vain, we tried to explain. In vain, they tried to understand.

Their skepticism had the effect of throwing down the gauntlet to my faith. The only way to demonstrate that we were being led of the Lord was to allow God to show Himself strong by providing for *all* our needs. It was simple: if He supplied all that we needed, then it was God's will that we go. If not, then we were mistaken.

And we had a long list of needs! From a twelve-passenger van to a grain grinder, from a cargo trailer to a pressure cooker, from homeschooling books to a new computer—we needed tons of stuff before we could head out. There was certainly no shortage of opportunities for God to prove His leading.

In those months of preparation to leave for Oaxaca, my prayer life became stronger than perhaps ever before. It had to be...I knew that this whole venture was going to be a major challenge to my faith. Familiar scripture verses took on whole new meaning in those days...

One of my journal entries at the time focused on Isaiah 8:18:

> *"Here am I, and the children whom the Lord has given me! We are for signs and wonders in Israel, from the Lord of Hosts, who dwells in Mount Zion."(NKJV)*
>
> *Yes, Lord, here we are, we and the children You have given us. People stare at us in wonder, wondering how we could possibly be so crazy as to pursue such a course with seven children. And it* is *crazy, I admit. Not to mention exceedingly difficult. And* impossible.

So it will be very embarrassing if You don't come through. I mean, we can survive embarrassment and humiliation, but what about Your holy Name? That should not happen. Lord, You who dwell in Zion, show Yourself strong and mighty. Show Yourself as the Lord of Hosts, able to lead, able to provide. Receive praise and honor and glory through our lives and those of the children You have given us!"

In March and April of 2001, we jumped through the hoops of applying and joining Missionary Ventures, our Florida-based mission. Then we hit the road to share our vision and the needs of Oaxaca with interested groups and churches.

To the uninitiated, this process goes by various monikers, each one cleverly designed to disguise its actual purpose. 'Deputation,' 'partnership development,' 'support discovery'—each one of these labels is a flimsy disguise for the process of raising enough funds to send missionaries on their way. Regardless of whatever innocuous-sounding name it might have, this fund-raising frenzy is not always a pleasant experience for the missionaries involved. Sometimes it can get downright ugly!

One day we were sitting around our huge kitchen table, the entire surface littered with stacks and stacks of letters, envelopes, prayer cards, and stamps. Ellie and I, along with four or five of our older kids, were plowing through lists of financial supporters, prayer supporters, *possible* financial and prayer supporters, and people who would never support us in any way if their lives depended on it. We were also trying to sort out letters to Canadians, letters to Americans and letters to all other countries. It was a mess, and the harder we tried to achieve some kind of order, the messier it got.

Suddenly, something in me snapped and I just started yelling. Basically, it was along these lines: "What's the *matter* with you stupid kids?! I thought some of you would have the gift of organization! We need help here! Why can't somebody get us *organized*?!" Ellie and the kids just stared at me aghast as I continued to rant and rave. It wasn't their fault that our family is not known for being a model of efficiency, but I was so frustrated and stressed that I lashed out, wanting to blame anybody. So I blamed our poor kids who were just doing the best they could.

Eventually Ellie calmed me down and made me go have a nap, and somehow or other they managed to sort out the mess. Peace was restored, but the strain of deputation was obviously taking its toll.

It took six months from the time we set our sights towards Oaxaca until the day we were ready to leave. Through prayer and God's faithfulness (not my faith or organizational skills), gradually all the pieces fell into place. God provided financial partners to stand with us, and He raised up a prayer team to empower us. He supplied the schoolbooks, the pressure cooker, the computer, and all the other out-going supplies on our list. He even provided a big, beautiful, like-new cargo trailer! There were many times during those six months that I was tempted to give up in despair, but then another answer to prayer would come through. How could I doubt His leading with all these reassuring signposts along the way?

There was just one thing lacking—the biggest obstacle both to us and to our skeptical friends. We still had no reliable transportation. Our van was only an eight-seater, and there were nine of us. Even worse, it was way too old and had way too many miles on it. Ted, our excellent mechanic friend, warned us that it probably wouldn't even make it out of Oregon, let alone all the way to Mexico. It was obvious that we weren't going *anywhere* unless God came through in the transportation department as well.

Post-Pedestal Pondering

There will be times in your ministry when your loved ones (not just your mother) will affirm, applaud, and approve the choices you make. However, there may also come a time when God calls you to walk a path that is not understood by others. He may ask you to go way out on a limb for Him, with no guarantee that the limb can support your weight. It is unlikely that God will grant your friends and relatives a special revelation of His purposes in your life, and so they may register concern or even alarm at the direction you are taking. Walking in faith while facing such a reaction from others can be a real struggle.

With God's proven track record of faithfulness throughout all of our previous years of ministry, it should have been easy for me to trust Him in this new adventure. Even so, I went through a major struggle to keep faith while we waited for God to supply our needs. If (when!) you go through a similar challenge to your faith, remember that:

- You need the blessing of your spiritual authorities

- Your other friends and loved ones may not understand

- The skepticism of others should not deter you from obedience to God's call

- The skepticism of others should prompt you to examine and confirm God's leading in your life

- Transition times tend to be chaotic and stressful

- God is quite capable of guiding you through the withholding or the provision of His supply

Perhaps friends who love you and are concerned for your sanity have already labeled you a 'fool.' While it is okay to be a 'fool for Christ,' it is never okay to be a simple and presumptuous fool. Don't become defensive if your loved ones are playing the role of Mr. Spock in your life. When they point out that your course of action is illogical, they may be right. Mr. Spock's logical counsel often prevented disaster for the Starship *Enterprise*. On the other hand, there were times when Captain Kirk's seemingly reckless and unreasonable course of action saved the galaxy! The important thing to discern is whether, at *this* moment, God is asking you to be an illogical fool for Him or a reasonable fool for Him. However He leads you, follow the path in faith and humility.

CHAPTER TEN

A Tale of Two Vans

The chariots of God are tens of
thousands and thousands of thousands.
Psalm 68:17a

There we were, ready to leave, with almost everything in place—everything except a van. The saying "All dressed up and no place to go" certainly took on a new significance for us. I am aware that God often delays His answers to prayer, but as we waited for God to drop a van out of the sky for our trip to Oaxaca, I begged Him repeatedly to break protocol and make an exception for us. But as the weeks went by, I began to doubt whether God was going to answer our prayers at *all*...last minute or otherwise.

It felt like this whole endeavor of heading to Oaxaca was progressing rapidly from the sublime to the ridiculous. One of my journal entries from that time reflected my growing embarrassment:

> *Father, today the doubts have hit me full force,*
> *starting with my friend's question of, "Do we have a*

plan in place in the event that God doesn't supply a van?" Well, no, we don't have a plan—except to wait. Of course, we can't buy a van—we have no money, and we can't go into debt. So our only plan is to wait. And how stupid does that look? What foolishness! "This man began to build and was not able to finish!" Oh Lord, up until now I had such peace. Peace that we were in Your will; peace that You wanted us to keep pressing on and preparing as if we will have a van by the day we're ready to leave. But now I feel like an idiot—like a laughingstock to everyone. Everyone keeps asking when we're leaving and I don't know what to say. I was embarrassed going to McIsaac's grocery store today, thinking people were laughing at me. I was reluctant to talk to Rita when I got my hair done, and even felt stupid talking to Heather on the phone. Have we painted ourselves into a corner here? Are we fools playing out a comedy of errors? Are You going to provide a van for us to go, or are we going to provide fuel for gossip, laughter and mockery for the whole community and beyond? Lord, I do believe You are calling us to Oaxaca, but where is Your provision? We are spending money hand over fist buying our outgoing supplies. But are we really going? We've torn apart our house sorting and packing. But are we going to stay? God, we can't do this on our own. Please show up!

Still no sign of a van.

The day came when we had to move out of our house to make room for the renters who were moving in. That night while the kids slept on mattresses on the floor, I walked through the house crying. *What on earth are we doing to our poor children? We are removing all their security, pushing them out of their nest without any guarantee that they can fly! Are we out of our minds, or is God really in this?* That night as I wept for my children, I honestly didn't know.

The next day we left on vacation. The good folks at Cannon Beach Conference Center had granted us a scholarship, so we headed off for a week at the beach. After all the work and stress of deputation and packing, we really needed a break. The glitch was that following our week of vacation, we would have nowhere to live. Without a van, we couldn't leave for Mexico. Without a house, we couldn't go back home.

We recognized God's voice nudging us to give up the security of our home *before* we saw Him supply a van, but it still felt crazy and irresponsible and embarrassing. I was worried that we were going to finish our vacation and then languish in somebody's backyard for the rest of the summer. I was afraid that people would hold us up as examples of foolishness in serving God.

On the one hand, God was telling me not to worry about mundane things like shelter, food, clothing, and vans. On the other hand, to my way of thinking, there was a fine line between not worrying about them and being totally irresponsible. *Have we crossed that line? Is God going to bless our steps of faith, or are we just presumptuous fools after all?*

Wednesday at Cannon Beach came and went, then Thursday, and there was still no answer. On Saturday our vacation would be over, and where would we go then?

It was lunchtime on Friday, and our family was eating sandwiches when Tom Thornton, an old friend from our Multnomah college days approached us. He said, "I have something that you need, and you have something that I need." He went on to explain that since he had a twelve-passenger Dodge van and we had an eight-passenger Dodge van, we should just trade! His family didn't need such a big van, he said, and our family did. Of course, it wasn't at all a fair trade. He was a mechanic, and his van was newer and kept in tip-top shape. Our van left a lot to be desired, to be sure, but Tom already knew that. Nevertheless, he and his wife Deanne felt led of the Lord to offer us their van, and they urged us to accept.

Well, naturally, it didn't take much to persuade us at that point. We were totally elated as Tom showed us his van, and we made plans to trade titles. At last, God had come through! He had supplied a van for us, and we could soon be on our way to Mexico! God had finally answered our months and months of prayer—at the last minute—but He had answered, and answered well.

We walked around on cloud nine all afternoon that Friday at the beach. At seven o' clock that evening, though, something even more incredible happened. We received a phone call from a pastor back in Hood River. Apparently, there was a couple in his church who had a twelve-passenger Ford van that they wanted to give us! It also was in great shape with very low mileage. Did we want it? Ellie didn't know how to explain that we had already received a Dodge twelve-seater van that very same day!

Now what were we to do? Our pastor friend gave Ellie this advice: "Bring the Dodge back to Hood River, pick up the Ford and have both vans examined by a mechanic. Then you can choose the best one and be on your way." It sounded reasonable, so we agreed to that plan.

That night, as we lay in bed, trying to sleep, we could hardly believe what God had done. Within the space of twenty-four hours, He had provided not one, but two vans! Now we had vans coming out of our ears. God obviously has a sense of humor, and was proving to us that there is no shortage of vans in His department.

Over the next few days, our mechanic friend examined both vans and pronounced them both in good shape and equally sound. With no obvious first choice of which van to take, we were totally perplexed...now what were we supposed to do?

At that point we were staying with Pastor Don and Ruth Gibbs, dear friends who had opened their home to us while we finished up the last- minute details getting ready to leave. We shared our bewilderment with them, and they pointed out an obvious solution. "Just take both vans! Then you won't be so squished on the trip to Mexico, and you can sell one of the vans later." Their suggestion rang true, and so that's what we did. Within days we hit the road for Mexico with both vans loaded to the gills, and the Dodge van pulling the cargo trailer.

God had called us to set out on a 'pilgrimage' to Oaxaca. We obeyed, but my faith had faltered many times in the process. Like most missionaries, we are not giants of faith—just ordinary people with wobbly faith whom God calls to do a particular job.

As we waved goodbye to family and friends, we were amazed at all that God had done. The impossible had happened—God had supplied for all our needs, above and beyond all that we could have asked or thought! Our reputation as slightly crazy missionary types was probably confirmed in the minds of many, but God's reputation as Jehovah Jireh, our Provider, was intact. In spite of my whining, my doubts and my lack of faith, He had proved Himself faithful again! How could I not trust Him for the journey that lay ahead?

Post-Pedestal Pondering

If God has been leading you on a walk of faith for any length of time, you know by now that He is able to provide anything, anywhere, anytime. However, you are probably also aware of an irritating little tendency of His to delay answers to prayer until the very last minute. Perhaps it is because He likes His children to exercise faith over a prolonged period of time and in so doing to stretch their spiritual muscles. Perhaps

He gets more glory by coming through with an answer to prayer when is seems that all hope is already gone. Whatever the reasons for this particular strategy, He has used it time and time again in our ministry experience.

I hope that when you struggle with your faith and your patience, you can be encouraged by the fact that you are not alone. Even though I know full well God's typical strategy of delayed provision, the inevitable wait still tends to chip away at my fragile faith. Maybe it's only the George Müellers among us (of whose company I am not one), who can look unflinchingly into the face of God's apparent procrastination. Me? I blink every time. I guess that's why God has to teach me the same lessons over and over again. I have such a short retention span!

So for my benefit as much as yours, let's review. God will:

- Frequently (always?!) delay answers to prayer until the last minute

- Sometimes delay past the point of our public embarrassment

- Stretch our faith by delaying

- Provide abundantly well

- Take us through the same lessons over and over again (until we get it, I guess)

- Always prove faithful

Remember that God knows you inside and out. If you doubt His ability to supply your needs, and supply them on time, then don't be surprised if He custom designs a little faith-stretching exercise for your exclusive benefit. He loves you too much to leave you in doubt.

Pop Quiz Number Two

Choose the correct letter to fill in each blank:

1. *God frequently tests our faith using the following device:* _____

   a. Answering our prayers according to our timetable
   b. Instant gratification
   c. Apparent procrastination

2. *Full-time Christian workers have* _____ *faith just like other Christians.*

   a. Unshakable
   b. Giant-sized
   c. Sometimes wobbly

3. *God is always* _____.

   a. Ambivalent
   b. Devious
   c. Faithful

By now the answers to the above questions should be so obvious that I'm not even going to bother giving them to you.

However, if you're unsure of your score, then go back and re-read the last few chapters till you can answer each question with total confidence. If, after several attempts you are still confused, then I will consider myself to have failed in my mandate. Please don't let me know—I'm too insecure to handle such devastating news.

CHAPTER ELEVEN

Getting There is
Half the Fun!
or Road Trip from Hell

*When you pass through the waters, I will be
with you; and when you pass through the rivers,
they will not sweep over you. When you walk
through the fire, you will not be burned;
the flames will not set you ablaze.*
Isaiah 43:2

Have you ever seen *National Lampoon's Vacation*? It is a movie that I heartily "disrecommend" on a number of counts. However, if you've seen it, you will for sure think twice before setting out on a long road trip with the family just for fun. In the movie, everything that was possible to go wrong did...and more besides! It proved to be a disastrous vacation—one which Chevy Chase's character and his family never wished to repeat.

99

I know a sure-fire cure for anyone who has ever been tempted to pedestalize full-time Christian workers. Let them be a fly on the wall of the van as said Christian workers set off on a four thousand-mile trip with seven kids in tow. The fly's disillusionment will be swift and it will be complete. I'm just so thankful that no one was along to witness our fallen human natures hanging out all over the place on that first trip to Oaxaca. It was not a pretty sight.

Oh, the first day wasn't so bad...maybe because we only traveled three hours to Bend, Oregon, where we stayed the night at a nice hotel compliments of a friend. Over hamburgers at Burger King, we congratulated ourselves on *finally* starting out for Mexico, and then swam all evening in the hotel pool. So far, so good.

The next day it seemed to take hours to pack and get ready to go. It was then that I discovered I had misplaced my curling iron. Well naturally, no self-respecting woman can go far without doing her hair—even if she is a missionary. Of course, the whole family, the two vans, and the cargo trailer had to wait in the parking lot while I indulged my vanity and went shopping for a curling iron!

The good news is that it didn't take long. The bad news is that while they were waiting for me, some child (who shall remain anonymous) yanked too hard on the sliding door of the Ford van, and the door fell off. It was unfixable without a major welding job, so from that day on, the door on that van had to remain locked shut all the way from Oregon to Mexico. The passengers were forced to clamber in and out over the front seats. Ellie was not happy.

In spite of that somewhat inauspicious beginning, the trip went fairly smoothly for the first couple of days. I had a Rubbermaid tub stocked with surprise toys, games, and story tapes to be brought out at judicious moments. I basically dedicated myself full-time to entertaining the little guys, while Ellie and sixteen-year-old Caleb each dedicated themselves full-time to driving a van.

Ellie and I had decided that the best way to tackle the trip was to break it up into very small, manageable chunks. Our plan was never to travel more than seven or eight hours a day, so as not to wear out the children. We also planned to find some kind of fun activity each evening after traveling to reward the kids for their patient endurance of the long hours on the road. It was a good plan. It was also very stupid.

Neither Ellie nor I are known for our mathematical prowess. What we had failed to calculate was exactly how *long* a journey of four thousand miles would take at only seven or eight hours a day. We were so concerned about not embittering the children who were suffering such a long trip, that we didn't take into account how much longer we were making the trip by going at such a slow rate.

Blissfully ignorant of that little detail, on the third night we made it to San Jose, California, where we stayed overnight with very kind and generous friends. We were enjoying their warm hospitality so much that we hated to leave the next morning. As Ellie and the older kids were saying their goodbyes in the driveway, I ran back into the house for one last check to make sure we hadn't forgotten anything.

I returned just in time to see baby Esther with both legs straddling the back wheel of the car that Mrs. D. had just pulled into the garage! The car was still running, and the dear lady was behind the wheel with no idea that Esther was within an inch of being crushed. I let out a blood-curdling scream as I ran towards her. Ellie and Mr. D. also saw the situation and started yelling to Mrs. D. to stop the car and not move at all. We pulled Esther out from around the tire and she was unscathed, but a bit bewildered about why all the grown-ups were screaming and sweating!

No one had seen how it happened, but somehow Esther had been toddling along and had fallen, or had deliberately paused to inspect the wheels of the pretty car purring so nicely in the driveway. It was truly gut-wrenching to consider how close our baby's life had come to being snuffed out.

We determined never to relax our guard on our kids from that moment on. What we didn't realize was that the endless deserts of New Mexico, Arizona, and Texas can lull even the best-intentioned parents into a hazy stupor.

The heat and unchanging flat sameness of the desert made for sheer boredom much of the time. Of course, it was not unendurable—it was just terribly monotonous. By God's grace, we survived the boredom and the bickering all the way to San Antonio, Texas. There we visited the Alamo, which was interesting although excruciatingly hot to our northern-born bodies.

We were some hours south of San Antonio when something happened to break up the relentless monotony.

As you remember, we were driving two vehicles; therefore, we had walkie-talkies to communicate between us. After stopping for gas and potty breaks, Ellie always talked to Caleb on the radio checking to make sure that we had everybody. For example, he would say: "Okay, I have Mum, Isaac, Johanna, and Esther. Do you have Josh, Lucas and Benjamin?" Without fail, he went through this little ritual while heading back to the main highway. Except this one time.

On that fateful day, we stopped for gas and then continued on down the road for half an hour or so till we came to a Pizza Hut. Absolutely totally *sick* of McDonald's and peanut butter sandwiches by that time, we all voted for the treat of a sit-down pizza meal. Better yet, there was even a salad bar, which Ellie and I enjoyed while all the kids played video games in a little room in the corner of the restaurant.

Eventually the pizza came, and Ellie called the kids to come and say grace. Everyone came except for Isaac, so we sent Lucas back to the video room to tell him to get over here and pray with us. Lucas came back saying that Isaac wasn't there. With a sickening suspicion that Isaac was sleeping in the stifling hot van, we sent Josh to wake him up. When he returned without Isaac, my blood ran cold as I realized that we must have left him behind at the last gas station!

In a panic, I dashed to use the restaurant phone while Ellie jumped in one of the vans to retrace our steps. I called 911 and stammered to the dispatcher that we had left our eight-year-old son at a gas station miles back! The woman on the phone informed me that they had already received a call from the station attendants who were with Isaac, waiting for us to come back. Ellie arrived there in double-quick time, rescued Isaac, and returned to meet the rest of us waiting at Pizza Hut.

Isaac was still shaken as he related, "I came out of the bathroom to get in the van, but it wasn't there! I saw both the vans driving away, and I ran after you waving my arms, but you didn't see me. I started crying and went to the gas station across the highway. The people there called the police and let me play with their turtles while I waited for you to come back. Why didn't you just wait for me?"

Ellie and I were stricken with remorse as we contemplated the many horrible fates that could have befallen our gentle son. We hugged him, asked forgiveness, and reassured him of our love for him. In private, though, we considered that of all of our children, sensitive Isaac was the worst possible one to have been left behind. We worried that he would be forever traumatized by his harrowing experience. Nevertheless, he seemed to bounce back quickly when once again in the bosom of his large, loving, and boisterous family.

Later Ellie asked Isaac what he would have done if we hadn't come back. He said, "Well, I knew we were going to Oaxaca, so I would have just gone to Oaxaca and found you." Such is the confidence of an eight-year-old!

Now, I know, of course, that maybe *you* would never leave a child behind at a gas station in the middle of nowhere. Maybe you can prolong your perch on the pedestal, but we absent-minded missionaries certainly can't. In fact, not even the befuddled parents of Jesus belong on a pedestal. After all, they left their twelve-year-old son behind in Jerusalem while they traveled on. With all their other children to worry about, it was three whole days before they really noticed that he was missing!

What kind of parent could do such a thing, you ask? Any well-meaning parent who dearly loves their child...but sometimes forgets him! Perhaps God had just such a scenario in mind when He said, *"Can a mother forget the baby at her breast and have no compassion on the child she has borne? Though she may forget, I will not forget you! See, I have engraved you on the palms of my hands."* (Isaiah 49:15,16) Hard to forget someone engraved into your very flesh!

Arriving in the Rio Grande Valley of Texas, we spent a few days touching base with Ellie's extended family and getting our ducks in a row to cross into Mexico. Ellie's cousin Becky took me on a last-minute shopping trip to the last American mall before hitting the border. We were just going through an intersection when suddenly — WHAM! — we were broadsided by a car turning left. Becky went into shock, while I tried to figure out if either one of us was hurt.

As we sped off to the hospital in the ambulance, I pretty much concluded that apart from some bruises and stiffness, miraculously, we were going to be just fine. Of course, it took tons of paperwork, hours of waiting for various and sundry tests, and hundreds of dollars for the medical staff to reach the same conclusion. But reach it they did, and we were finally released to go back to Becky's house to lie on her bed and nurse our wounds for the evening. Although we were relatively unscathed, Becky's van was totaled. Seeing it the next day, we were so grateful to God for allowing us to walk away from an accident that could have claimed our lives.

After experiencing three near tragedies in such close succession, it gradually began to seep into our consciousness that perhaps there was something sinister about this whole thing. We were on our way to Oaxaca, which has the largest concentration of unreached people groups in the Western Hemisphere. Satan has long been the undisputed sovereign there. Although we were just one family bringing light to the lost souls of Oaxaca, we did represent a significant threat to the dominion of darkness. Maybe we had underestimated the strategic impact of the war that we were entering. Apparently the enemy would stop at nothing to prevent us from even arriving intact at the battle scene!

Regardless of whatever nasty spiritual forces may have been arrayed against us, after crossing the border, we continued on our merry way until we reached the city of Tampico, Mexico. We timed our arrival just perfectly to coincide with nightfall, in order to hit every one of the hundreds of potholes lurking in the dark at the entrance to the city. Next, we succeeded in getting lost. After that we got stuck in a horrendous traffic jam in the downtown core, caused by none other than our own vans and cargo trailer. (I won't even mention the bribe that we were forced to pay a corrupt policeman to extract ourselves from that situation.)

When we finally checked into a decent hotel, the kids were pretty much bouncing off the walls from the hours of delay. Ellie and I had reached a semi-catatonic state, neither knowing nor caring what the kids were doing...until Benjamin almost choked to death.

After days of drinking warm bottled water in the van, the children were delighted to find an ice machine down the hall from us. Benjamin had discovered that the little round pieces of ice were perfect for sucking on while jumping on the bed! Unless, of course, one wants to stay alive. The ice was just the right size to wedge sideways in his little throat and he was already turning color when I noticed him choking! No amount of backslapping would dislodge the ice, and I was loath to try the Heimlich Maneuver on him for fear I would crack a rib. Still, the alternative outcome was not a happy one, so finally in desperation I used the Heimlich, and the ice popped right out. Benjamin was gasping for air, while I went limp with relief and the after-effects of an adrenaline rush.

Now I realize, of course, that Benjy should never have been jumping on the bed in the first place and that this whole incident could have been avoided. Under normal circumstances, we would never have allowed jumping on a hotel bed. What I would like to point out, however, is that being cooped up in a van for long hours every day for days on end is not a normal circumstance for an energetic four-year-old boy. And the exhaustion that the boy's road-weary parents were experiencing was also an unusual occurrence. There is nothing *normal* about traveling for thousands of miles with seven kids in tow! So, yes, we *were* irresponsible to have allowed ice-sucking bed-jumping activities, but that night we were truly past the point of being responsible for much of anything.

At this point you may be thinking that each of these unhappy incidents was the result of parental inattentiveness—nothing more. You may be right at that. We were certainly distracted and preoccupied. However, I suspect that there was a little more to it than that. I don't think that during the summer's journey, Ellie and I suddenly morphed into criminally neglectful parents. My suspicion is that our enemy, the devil, was actively prowling around like a roaring lion seeking whom he could devour. Recognizing our vulnerability and weariness on such a long journey, he leaped to the offensive!

I hope you can see from this that when it comes to recognizing our own place in the cosmic struggle, we missionaries and pastors can be incredibly dense. Perhaps the obstacles that we were experiencing should have been patently obvious as the enemy's ploy to defeat us before we even arrived in Oaxaca. But even after four close calls, we only dimly perceived that we were caught in the cross hairs of Satan's scope.

Of course, we were praying for God's protection all along the trip, and maybe after these close calls we beefed up our prayer life a bit. However, I know that we didn't actively enter into serious intercession for the remaining hundreds of miles. We were still in survival mode only – just trying to endure the heat and the hundreds of potty stops. For the kids' sake, we were also trying to remain relatively cheerful and avoid snapping each other's heads off in all the stress of traveling. Who had energy left for entering into heavy spiritual warfare?

As it turned out, our snail's pace strategy for covering the miles did eventually get us to Oaxaca—*twenty-five* days after setting out from Oregon! We had stopped and visited friends and relatives here and there, and what with one thing and another, the journey took a ridiculously long time. By the night that we finally arrived in Mitla, Oaxaca, I was gritting my teeth just to keep from screaming. I felt like I would go mad if we had to stay cooped up in the van for even one more hour! There was nothing so wonderful and welcoming as the cozy guest apartment at the missionary center where we stayed when we first arrived.

Even though Satan had failed to prevent us from reaching our destination, he still had one more trick up his sleeve to try to take us out. On our very first day in Mitla, some gracious and hospitable new friends invited us over for lunch. After we had eaten, they were kind enough to give our kids turns riding their horse. While Ellie and I were standing and chatting with our hosts on their patio, we heard a strange choking noise behind us. Whipping around, we saw Benjamin dangling by his neck from a noose!

Ellie grabbed him and instantly loosened him from the noose, but it was the most awful sight to have seen. The only thing that saved Benjamin from death by hanging was that his fingers were wedged in under the rope giving him a tiny bit of room to breathe and hold himself up.

Being horsey people, our friends normally had their saddle hanging from the handy noose on the patio. Benjamin simply hadn't been able to resist the temptation of a dangling rope, and had pushed a chair up to the noose and put it around his neck. Suddenly he slipped, the chair fell out from under him and he was suspended in midair until we heard him struggling for his life! Once again, by God's grace, a terrible tragedy had been averted in the nick of time.

Thankfully, the road trip was now officially over. The extenuating circumstances of interminable travel and the ensuing exhaustion and weakness came to an end. So did the repeated attacks on our lives.

As we settled into life in Oaxaca, we became very aware of the enemy's stronghold on that area of Mexico. The spiritual bondage that the people there are under is blatantly obvious, warning us to be ever on the alert to resist the attacks of the enemy.

This is not to say, however, that we are always ready and able to wrestle against the rulers of the darkness of this age. There are many occasions when our resistance wears thin and we succumb to discouragement and the various sneaky tactics of Satan. My spiritual armor is frequently rusty and unwieldy and I feel more like the Tin Man in *The Wizard of Oz* than a lean, mean prayer machine.

Even a cursory perusal of Ephesians 6 is enough to remind me that I do not belong on any pedestal. It is not my great spiritual strength that enables us to withstand in the evil day, and having done all to stand. No, I believe that for Ellie and me both, any success on the field is due mostly to our praying mothers and the whole army of prayer warriors that God has raised up to stand behind us. Without the faithful prayers of others, I'm sure that we would be rendered useless. And I suspect that is the case with most of us in ministry. Yes, we are in the battle full-time, but that does not mean we deserve to be put on a pedestal. Only that we desperately need the prayers of God's people!

Post-Pedestal Pondering

At times it is necessary to travel long distances on the road (or by plane or canoe) — not on vacation, but for ministry purposes. Such trips are way down on my list of fun things to do, but sometimes they are unavoidable. When we must go, at least we can go in the confidence that God will be with us, and He will protect us, come what may.

Maybe you're not facing an interminable road trip any time in the near future. But it is for certain sure that Satan will concoct something from the pit of hell to try to sideline you from effective ministry. A church split, a death in the family, a forced evacuation from your host country, a nasty divorce of dear friends — something will happen!

When you are facing these stressful times that try men's souls, it is important to:

- Recognize that you are in the battle zone

- Avoid picking fights with your spouse or ministry partner

- Not beat yourself up for your lack of energy/your preoccupation/your irresponsibility

- Enlist *tons* of prayer support

- Keep going!

Remember that the floodwaters will eventually recede; the fires will eventually die down. These intense times do not last forever. While you are under attack and vulnerable, cling to God's promises of protection and *don't give up*!

CHAPTER TWELVE

Culture Shock...or
the Lack Thereof

Here there is no Greek or Jew, circumcised or
uncircumcised, barbarian, Scythian, slave or free,
but Christ is all, and is in all.
Colossians 3:11

B ear with me for a minute while I interrupt the story to
lay a necessary foundation for this chapter.

In the shrinking "global village" that we all live in, we can
go out for dinner and sample Chinese, East Indian, Mexican,
Mongolian, or Thai cuisine. We can learn French, German, or
Spanish at local community education centers. We can even
participate in a student-exchange program or a short-term
mission trip to Romania, Guatemala, or Zambia. All of this
cross-cultural mingling greatly enhances and enriches our
lives. But what happens when, instead of engaging the other
culture on our own turf, or on a two-week mission trip, we
actually make a long-term commitment? How do we cope

when we find ourselves strangers in a strange land—and that land is supposed to become our new home?

Engaging a new culture in such an 'up close and personal' way often brings out some distressing emotions—commonly referred to as culture shock. Customs and traditions of the host culture that were quaintly charming when viewed from a distance begin to grate on our nerves. Racial prejudices that we had always eschewed begin to seep into our thinking. We react to minor irritations with major hostility. We feel disgust, anger, and even hatred for the people with whom we came to share the love of Christ.

In our emotional confusion, it is comforting to realize that the barriers between cultures will eventually melt away when Christ is exalted above all. Racial distinctions will become completely insignificant when we all bow together before the throne of our Lord Jesus. But in the meantime, we somehow have to survive the onslaught of culture shock.

I never fail to be amused when Americans or Canadians with little or no previous cross-cultural experience come to visit us in Oaxaca. Overwhelmed and bewildered by the multitude of cultural differences that they are bumping up against, they often look to us for advice. It is not the stress that they are experiencing or their reactions to it that amuses me—it is the fact that they assume that veteran missionaries are exempt from such stress.

The reality is that anyone leaving Canada or the U.S. and attempting to integrate into the society of a developing country will experience some degree of culture shock. The only variables are the severity of the shock, the time that it hits, the duration, and what form it takes. No one can avoid it, thus no one should presume to be above such discomfort.

Now back to the story.

Before we left Oregon for Oaxaca, we pessimistically predicted that it would probably take a full two years before any of us would really feel at home in Mexico. Based on our disastrous two years in Guatemala, we prepared our children for the worst, and fully expected culture shock to hit us hard. Imagine, then, our surprise, when after about six weeks our kids were happily settled in as if they had lived there all their lives! They tackled the new culture with wonder and enthusiasm—setting the example for me to try to follow.

Although the transition to life in Mexico was at first relatively easy for the kids and me, Ellie was immediately plunged into a high-pressure situation guaranteed to blow anyone's top. The house we had rented was at first unfit for habitation. It took almost two months of hard work to get our house, affectionately dubbed 'The Money Pit,' to the livable stage. During that time we enjoyed the hospitality of the Wycliffe center, living in the same cozy duplex where we had stayed our first night in Mitla. None of us were really suffering—in fact, the kids and I were having a great time homeschooling, making new friends, and settling into life in Mexico. It was Ellie who first bore the brunt of the culture shock.

He went through sheer frustration dealing with the Mexican plumbers, tile-layers, electricians, and carpenters because:

a. None of them had phones, so Ellie had to track them down at their houses.

b. They said they would be there at 8:00 on Tuesday morning, while having no intention of showing up anytime within the next two months.

c. Their qualifications to actually do a job were sometimes based more on imagination than reality.

d. Once a job was actually begun, there was apparently no rush to finish it, judging by the fact that workers often disappeared for several days at a time in the middle of a project.

e. Since few, if any, of the contractors had vehicles, any supplies that were needed had to be sought, bought, and brought to the site by Ellie himself.

It was not a *bad* method of doing things...it was just different, as Ellie kept trying to remind himself. Even though he is Mexican by blood, he is U.S. born, and the relative inefficiency of the Mexican system offended his American sensibilities. He often came home angry and irritated by the daily challenges of this new system.

In spite of the endless frustrations and delays, the broken shower tiles were finally fixed, a new shower floor was put in, the roof leaks were (mostly) repaired, a new kitchen sink cabinet was built to replace the termite-eaten one, the outdoor plumbing was replaced, new screens and door knobs were installed, broken windows repaired, overhanging trees de-limbed, drains unclogged, toilet fixed, bees-nests evacuated, cockroaches evicted, house painted, hot water-heater installed, gas tank and stove made (mostly) operational, a million holes in the walls patched and sealed, kitchen sink installed, old abandoned well covered with kid-proof concrete lid, etc. etc. etc.

Ellie valiantly struggled through this seven-week marathon of fixing-upping, and even lived to tell the tale. In the end, we were all rewarded with a clean, reasonably comfortable house to live in! Once we moved out of temporary housing and into our own place, Ellie was able to buckle down and learn the job in the recording studio that he had come to do. He became a much happier and much easier-to-live-with man—back to his normal easy-going self.

But there were other challenges to face in adjusting to our new life. I remember at first being horrified by the twenty huge vultures that came to roost in our trees every night. In the late afternoons they would return from their scavenging forays around Mitla, circling over our kids playing outside in the yard. As I nervously watched them wheeling ever lower and lower, I pictured one of them suddenly deciding to sample *live* little boy or girl instead of dead carrion. Each evening I would breathe a sigh of relief when the big black monsters would finally settle down to roost.

Over time, however, my apprehension in the presence of the filthy, disease-carrying birds gave way to a strange kind of affection for them. Eventually I came to think of them as our pet vultures that faithfully returned home to the fold each evening. It was kind of a cozy feeling, like the cows returning home to the barn for their evening milking. One night the vultures failed to come home, and I was genuinely sad to realize that they had decided to find a quieter spot to live.

That's the way culture shock often goes: what starts out as dismay and disgust at some aspect of the new culture eventually gives way to a strange kind of affection and pride. Reaching that point of adjustment does not necessarily mean that you have arrived...only that you're well on your way.

Another point of stress was learning to deal with scorpions, snakes, spiders, and other dangerous nasties. Long-term missionaries just take these things in stride, but they can really throw rookies for a loop.

One night while Ellie was away on a village trip, I came wide awake to see a huge tarantula the size of my hand dangling over my bed! I jumped out of bed and turned on the light...and the thing disappeared. Which leads me to believe that maybe it was never really there...except in my imagination. (Come to think of it, that same gigantic spider put in an appearance almost every time that Ellie was gone overnight.) Nevertheless, I immediately dug out a roll of duct tape and feverishly set to work patching several gaping holes in our ceiling. One can never be too certain, can one? Besides, the effect was so aesthetically pleasing that I only wished I had duct-taped the ceiling months earlier.

In spite of my best artistic efforts, I spent a restless night, and as morning approached, I felt exhausted. My alarm was set for 6:00, but I decided to turn it off and sleep in till at least 7:00—foregoing my cherished time with the Lord. Wouldn't you know it—at 6 a.m. *on the dot* an earthquake struck! I was jolted wide- awake, praying for protection all the way through it, and then, of course, I couldn't go back to sleep. So I got up after all, and kept my appointment with God. Perhaps that was one of the purposes for the earthquake in the first place.

To be sure, even the kids had a few minor struggles in adjusting to our new life. Our fellow townspeople amazed all of us with their insatiable appetite for all-night partying. The incessant, unbelievably loud music would blare on all night, until six or seven a.m., sometimes several nights a week. In those first few months, our reaction to sleepless nights of horrible music was rage. One of us was always threatening to take a shotgun to the loudspeakers at the party sites. But the noise of parties all around us in the neighbor- hood paled in comparison to parties given by our neighbors just over our wall.

One evening as they warmed up for an all-nighter, our windows were literally rattling and our walls shaking from the incredible volume! Sitting at the same table in our house, we had to shout at each other to be heard.

Trying to be very diplomatic, I ventured over next door and offered congratulations for the glad event that they were celebrating (nephew's first communion, or some such thing). "Is the band going to play all night?" I inquired, and they responded, "Of course!"—proud to flaunt their status in being able to afford an all-night band. Then I tactfully mentioned that our walls were shaking and windows rattling from the deafening noise, to which our kind neighbors assured me in all sincerity, "Oh, don't worry—they won't fall down!"

In the face of such inability to comprehend that there was a problem with the music, our rage gradually gave way to a philosophical acceptance of the situation. Realizing that nothing we could say or do would ever improve things in the slightest, we learned to relax, laugh about it, and even enjoy the rare occasions when the band members actually sang on key. ("Hey, that's a good song...") Some of us also became heavily dependent on earplugs, although truth be told, now most of us just sleep right through the noise.

Since most of the adjustment challenges we faced were relatively painless, I thought that I had escaped almost unscathed by culture shock. But I was wrong. It wasn't that anything major came up; it was just that after a year and a half of thoroughly enjoying our life and ministry in Mexico, a lot of minor irritations slowly developed into major frustrations. As you can see by the following e-mail message that I sent to a friend, there was nothing seriously wrong. I just wasn't coping well anymore with the little things.

I had an attack of culture shock today. We were invited to stay overnight at a friend's place in Oaxaca so that the little kids could see the city at night and we could do some grocery shopping in the morning. It was a good plan but the roads in the city were all blocked off last night due to protesters so it took FOREVER to get anywhere and when we finally got to the zocalo (town square) it was crazy crowded and horrifically noisy and the kids just wanted to get out of there ASAP and so we went to stay at our friend's house and Esther fussed and cried much of the night with a bad reaction to the worm medicine she's on, and Ellie was attacked by something biting his feet during the night and found a tic on his pillow, and then in the morning come to find that our friend had invited a Mexican pastor and another missionary to have a meeting with Ellie while he was in the city, so I spent the morning cleaning the friend's house while

Ellie had a long meeting and the kids just all sat around bored, and then we finally headed out through horrible traffic again and we went shopping and of course Sam's Club was out of milk and Soriana's milk all had an expiration date of tomorrow which means it's already sour and out of a stack of 200 notebooks only 5 of them were lined and all the rest were stupid graph paper but they're not sorted so I had to go through all 200 just to find the 5, and every single tag on the pants we were looking for Josh's birthday said the incorrect size, and the roads on the way back to Mitla are STILL torn up and I cried all the way home, and I'm disgusted with inefficiency and I WANT A BARBECUE GRILL! I'm venting. Can you tell? It would just be nice to take the family on a nice, easy, CONVENIENT outing without having to go through hell to do it. One bright spot was that we DID have running water for a change when we got back home. Small mercies.

We have learned that even the most well-adjusted missionaries occasionally go through periods when the cumulative stress of living and working in a foreign culture puts them over the edge for awhile. For me, sometimes the cure is to spend more time in prayer and Bible reading. At other times, what I need is a video night watching a chick flick like *Pride & Prejudice* while munching on chips and Canadian chocolate bars. Sometimes I just need to give myself permission to fall apart and cry for awhile. And sometimes the only real cure is to get away from the offending stresses for a few days in order to gain new perspective.

The important thing to realize is that while culture shock strikes at different times and in different ways, the certainty is that it *will* strike. No one need be ashamed of it…it is simply one of the stark realities of life in a foreign culture. And no one is exempt. Newcomers who are struggling to adjust and who are tempted to pedestalize veteran missionaries should resist the temptation. Even though the veterans might appear to be coping well today, tomorrow they may fall apart. All of us must live each day crying out to God for grace to cover a multitude of incomprehensible cultural differences.

Post-Pedestal Pondering

Are you anticipating an upcoming move to a foreign country? Or are you currently immersed in an unfamiliar culture and you feel like you're drowning? It will help you keep your head above water if you remember that culture shock:

- Is no respecter of persons

- Is inevitable

- Triggers disgust, anger, and sometimes hatred towards the host culture and members of it

- Is temporary, even though it seems to last forever

- May re-occur at unexpected intervals

- Will be completely eradicated at the coming of the Lord

In some ways, culture shock is like a semi-truck bearing down on you in a one-lane tunnel. You can't avoid being hit by it. Sometimes the only thing to do is to admit that you're crushed under the tires, keep a sense of humor, and eat chocolate!

CHAPTER THIRTEEN

A Painful Discovery — I Like Stuff

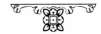

Do not store up for yourselves treasures on earth...
but store up for yourselves treasures in heaven...
for where your treasure is, there your heart will be also.
Matthew 6:19,20,21

I have many shortcomings, but I've always prided myself on the fact that at least I'm not materialistic! Or so I thought.

Financial worries were a major source of stress in our home during my growing-up years. Perhaps that's why I hated to spend money. I didn't want to cause any more stress. Rather than going out and buying new clothes, I usually waited until hand-me-downs found their way to me. I went away to college wearing my dad's old green sweater with my feet shod in his gray wool work socks. My American friends at college teased me about being a "northern frontierswoman," and they assumed that gray work socks must be a trademark of Canadian girls. In truth, I was just too cheap to buy new stuff.

I remember one day when Ellie and I were courting, and he went out and bought me an umbrella. I was grateful, but also shocked at his wasteful extravagance! I had survived the Portland rains just fine for three years at college without an umbrella, by simply running to catch up with someone who did have an umbrella.

One day there was an open house on campus, for visiting parents and friends. It was also the one day of the semester that the girls could tour the men's housing quarters and vice-versa (under supervision, of course). As I looked around Ellie's simple but neatly organized room, I couldn't help but notice another sign of wasteful extravagance: he had a *metal wastebasket* by his desk! *I* had always gotten by with using a brown paper bag for garbage. Obviously Ellie was a spend-thrift, judging by his trash receptacle. Perhaps this relationship wasn't going to work out, after all.

Seriously, I had three criteria for any man that I would consider marrying, besides that he must be heading into ministry.

> *1.* He should come from a big family (and want a big family!).
> *2.* He must be a hard worker.
> *3.* He should be poor.

In my mind, the three were interconnected, because if he came from a big family, chances are he'd most likely be poor, and being poor, chances are he'd have had to learn to work hard. To my way of thinking, poverty was a virtue that would go a long way towards warding off the evils of materialism.

Since we've been married, Ellie has sometimes been amused and sometimes frustrated by my dread of shopping. While he loves to window shop for fun, I can think of no greater waste of time than to look at stuff that I can't afford and don't need. I have always avoided shopping malls—

operating under the assumption that what I don't see, I won't covet. Mostly this strategy has worked.

Throughout all our years of ministry I was content with hand-me-down clothes, garage-sale furniture, and a ramshackle house. Then we moved to Mexico, and something in me changed. Little by little, all my suppressed materialistic urges came bubbling to the surface. Obviously I was not transformed into an avaricious money-grubber the instant my feet hit Mexican soil. No, it was a gradual process of learning to be discontent.

Mexico is a relatively poor country with an obvious distinction between the 'haves' and the 'have-nots.' Although I had lived my entire life striving for a simple lifestyle, upon arrival in Mexico I was automatically thrust into the category of the privileged upper class. It would have been useless to try to deny that we were rich...the proof of our wealth was sitting in our yard. Not only did we have a vehicle...we had two vehicles! In a country like Mexico, the possession of a car speaks volumes. Never mind that those two vehicles were both over thirteen years old and had been given to us.

Finding myself in a higher socio-economic bracket should have made me even more content than before, right? Yup...but that ain't how it happened! I realized that I had more stuff than many of my neighbors and friends around me, but that knowledge didn't breed contentment. You see, I wanted to create a lovely home for my family (which, by the way, is a perfectly acceptable desire for any godly woman to have). I wanted our home to be warm and cozy and comfortable...a beautifully soothing environment for family and friends to enjoy. Trouble was, I had no money to work with. While we were undeniably wealthy by most Mexican standards, we were undeniably broke most of the time.

As I struggled to get set up in housekeeping on a very limited budget, I was so grateful for the generous help that Jim and Jamie Loker provided. They shared tables, chairs, beds, and even kitchen cabinets with us. They bent over backwards to help us get settled in. Thanks to their help, we slowly made progress in the 'cute and cozy' department, but I was still not satisfied. I wanted to do more. How could I properly furnish a home without the garage-sale option? How could I decorate without tons of other peoples' cast-off treasures? I was stymied in my homemaking efforts by a chronic case of empty pocketbook.

To make matters worse, I remembered the message I once heard at a Christian ladies' conference. The speaker had waxed eloquent about the importance of making the master bedroom a lovely romantic haven at the end of the day. We were exhorted to create a quiet, soothing atmosphere with flowers, candles, etc. *Yeah right. We've been here in Oaxaca for eight months already, and we still can't even afford a bedroom door!* With or without flowers and candles, the lack of a door tended to put a real damper on romantic moods.

Please don't misunderstand me — I was not consumed by materialistic tendencies a hundred per cent of the time. Mostly, I was happy and fulfilled in our new ministry and our chosen lifestyle. By God's grace, I was usually able to face financial struggles philosophically and with a sense of humor.

For example, a certain son of ours once told me, "Mum, all my underwear has holes in it. I need some new underwear." I told him, "Sorry, son, but we don't have any extra money this month. You're going to have to wait till next month." He was okay with that, and waited patiently till we received our next financial disbursement.

Unfortunately, there was a shortage of funds again. Suspecting that some of our supporters had forgotten to give, I again told my son, "You're just going to have to wait a bit longer." He groaned, but of course he didn't have many options, so he waited.

A few weeks later he brought it up again. By that time there was enough money to buy underwear, but we were rushing around in a frenzy getting ready to leave on furlough. Every time I went shopping, (which, you will remember, was as seldom as possible), I forgot to buy him underwear. From that time on, it became a family joke. Each time he asked, I teasingly told him just to wait a while longer. I had underwear on my list and I *could* afford it, but it was kind of funny to watch him squirm. When his frustration level reached its absolute limit, I finally gave in and bought him his longed-for underwear!

While budget challenges had their funny side, once in a while I was overwhelmed by an unfamiliar attack of covetousness. "Why can't I have more stuff?" I demanded of God. "Why don't You supply more money so I can make a nicer home for my family? After all we've done for You," I accused, "why don't You do a better job in supplying our needs?"

I complained bitterly to God about how He could alleviate some of our financial strain, and yet He was choosing not to. I was like Topol in *Fiddler on the Roof,* who griped to God, "Would it spoil some vast eternal plan, if I were a wealthy man?"

In my weaker moments, I whined to God: "See how much I've sacrificed for You, God? What's in it for me? Where's the payback?" I was shocked by these ungodly attitudes that were seeping from my soul, but I felt powerless to stop them. The emotions of greed and selfishness simply rose unbidden from some ugly source deep inside me. I had thought that I was immune to the lure of materialism, but I was wrong. Give me a tiny bit of perceived deprivation, and I am just as susceptible as the next guy.

We faced a particularly lean month one December in Oaxaca. I was disappointed in the amount of support money sent to us, because I had somehow convinced myself that December would be a good month financially. With Christmas coming, I anticipated all sorts of extra goodies. When December's income turned out to be even worse than usual, I found myself identifying with Elisha's servant, Gehazi.

You remember the story: Naaman, the leprous Syrian, had followed the prophet Elisha's instructions to dip seven times in the Jordan River. When God healed him, Naaman was overcome with gratitude and wanted to bless Elisha with some kind of gift. Elisha refused any kind of monetary reward, but Gehazi, Elisha's servant, had other ideas.

Gehazi said to himself, "I will run after [Naaman] and get something from him." Gehazi deceitfully obtained two talents of silver and two sets of clothing from Naaman, but his windfall was short-lived. Elisha immediately confronted him with his greed and pronounced God's judgment on his sin.

"Is this the time to take money or to accept clothes, olive groves, vineyards, flocks, herds, or menservants and maidservants? Naaman's leprosy will cling to you and your descendants forever." (2 Kings 5)

My journal records my identification with Gehazi's greed:

To be truthful, Father, I thought it was going to be time to receive money and clothing, etc. this month. I thought that this month was going to be a month of financial blessing. I had expectations—even dreaming of rugs and a new couch and a space heater. But there is not enough for anything except to barely squeak by again. Oh Lord! This is bitter! I should not complain in any way, I know. You pour out Your blessing on us in so many other ways: children, health, friends, ministry and joy. Yet You do seem to withhold financial blessing from us, and to be honest, it is getting old. I am tired of the strain. I am tired of doing without. There! I said it! I want <u>stuff</u>! I want a decent floor and decent furniture. I want heat and light and water. I want a beautiful home. I am no better than Gehazi: I am greedy. My

*heart is not satisfied with the good gifts You have given.
I want more. So there You have it, Lord. I cannot hide
from You. You can see my desires and my struggle to
be content. Sure, I'm a missionary, and as such should
live above ' worldly desires' for material things. But I
don't, as You can see. My heart is bound to this earth,
and it is as selfish and greedy as anyone else's. I am
sorry to disappoint You, Father, but there it is. You may
as well strike me with leprosy too, for I am no better
than Gehazi. In fact, I'm probably worse.*

God, in His great mercy, did not instantly strike me with
leprosy. He gave me another chance...and another...and
another! I have still not completely conquered my lust for nice
stuff, and maybe I never will on this old earth. But as I struggle
to "seek first His kingdom and His righteousness," He patiently
forgives my ungodly lapses of materialism. He also delights in
surprising me with unexpected and undeserved little goodies.

That financially bleak December turned out to be not
so bleak after all. Eventually, the Holy Spirit convicted me
of my sin, and I repented of my selfishness. Soon after, we
found out that one of our supporting churches in Oregon had
sent us boxes and boxes of lovely Christmas gifts. Although
we could buy almost nothing in the way of gifts for each
other that year, we enjoyed a lavish Christmas extravaganza
of gifts for the whole family!

Post-Pedestal Pondering

Dr. Joe Aldrich was president of Multnomah School of the
Bible when I was in college. During chapel times, he used to
regale the student body with his hilarious collection of 'pithy
sayings.' One of Dr. Joe's favorites, as I recall, was this:

"You know, some people go into the ministry to do good,
and they end up doing very well indeed."

He was referring, of course, to those who somehow tap into a financially lucrative ministry situation, and end up comfortably set for life. In my experience, these situations are the exception rather than the rule. If you happen to be the host of your own Christian TV show, or are the pastor of a mega-church in California, you may be sitting pretty financially. But I'm afraid that most of us in ministry must battle the money demons on a fairly regular basis. It kind of goes with the territory.

I don't know of anyone who enters into vocational Christian service as part of a get-rich-quick scheme. If anyone does, chances are he will be bitterly disappointed. A basic axiom of the Christian faith is that you cannot serve both God and money. I'm sure that you believe and live by this axiom. Perhaps you have even sacrificed a good salary and a life of comfort in order to enter full-time ministry. You have counted the cost, put your hand to the plow, and have not looked back. But what happens when spiritual leaders *do* look back, and start to succumb to the seduction of materialism?

As a Christian leader, you may be tempted at times to complain to God about the sacrifices that you have made. No matter how diligently you have striven to put materialistic urges behind you, they have a nasty way of popping out unbidden. Don't be shocked by your human weakness…God isn't!

Remember that:

- You cannot serve both God and money

- No sacrifice that we make for God can compare with God's sacrifice of His Son

- Greed is a sin, no matter which way you slice it

- Unrepented sin brings punishment (Gehazi!)

- God is always ready to forgive

- God rewards His servants in unexpected ways, but not in response to selfish demands

When you succumb to the love of 'stuff,' allow God's Holy Spirit to convict and cleanse you. Then you will find that as you faithfully seek first God's Kingdom and His righteousness, all the stuff you really need will be added unto you!

"I am content with what I have,

Little be it, or much;

And, Lord, contentment still I crave

Because Thou lovest such.

Fullness to such a burden is

That go on pilgrimage;

Here little, and hereafter bliss,

Is best from age to age."

~John Bunyan

CHAPTER FOURTEEN

Furlough Fears and Frustrations

*For we do not preach ourselves, but Jesus
Christ as Lord, and ourselves as your
servants for Jesus' sake.*
2 Corinthians 4:5

If you are a missionary, then you are already aware of the
confusion that can result when you tell people that you are
'going on furlough.' Many people assume that (*a*) You are
quitting and leaving the mission field, or (*b*) You are taking
an extended vacation. The truth is actually (*c*) You are going
on home assignment to report back to your churches and to
raise necessary prayer and financial support.

Furlough is also a time for missionaries to renew ties with
family and friends, reconnect with the home culture, stock up
on supplies, and hopefully be refreshed spiritually. It can be a
time of tremendous blessing. Usually, however, it proves to be
a *mixed* blessing, due to circumstances beyond our control.

131

The challenge for missionaries is to view furlough as more than just a trial to endure. The challenge for pastors and other home-based spiritual leaders is to be sensitive to the needs of their returning missionaries, and to be ready to minister to them.

Due to the demanding regimen of frequent speaking engagements, furlough can be so physically and emotionally draining that sometimes a vacation is needed to recuperate *afterwards*. Recently we received an email from fellow missionaries who expressed their desire to move on to their new ministry assignment without the fatigue of a six-month furlough first. In their letter, the father wrote the following:

> *"But wait," you may say, "I thought a furlough was a rest time." No way! That is absolutely not the case. Maybe it was meant to be that, but we have found just the opposite. The last time we took a furlough, the family was so burnt out on ministry that I had to give them six months rest before I could ask them to be involved in a drama or do much in the way of music.*

This kind of exhaustion so typical of furlough is one reason why some missionaries dread the whole scene. I know a few who actually hate furlough time! I used to go so far as to think that the furlough and deputation systems were demonically inspired. Of course, I don't think that anymore (usually). I still recognize the shortcomings of the systems, but now I am content to allow God to redeem them. Just as He promised in Romans 8:28, *"...in all things God works for the good of those who love him, who have been called according to his purpose." All* things even includes the challenges of furlough and deputation time.

Before and during our first six-month furlough, I experienced a wide range of emotions related to this wild and wonderful time.

It began four or five months before we even left Mexico for our furlough. At that time, I felt so terribly dry spiritually that I was really worried. *How can I possibly go back to minister to our home churches and supporters when I feel like I have nothing to give?*

Our time in Mexico was a richly fulfilling time of ministry to others, but it was almost devoid of spiritual refreshment for me. I longed for meaningful worship services and challenging Bible teaching, but then I felt guilty for blaming the coldness of my heart on my physical and geographical circumstances. *I have the Word of God in my own language. I have the Holy Spirit. What more do I need? Why should I require more?*

My own motives were another major concern of mine as I anticipated our imminent return to Canada and the U.S. The fact was that we were under-supported, and really needed to beef up our financial base. But how could I impartially report on the needs of Oaxaca and give glory to God for all He had done while simultaneously trying to raise funds?

My prayer journal at the time reflected my concern:

Furlough. Deputation. Ay-yay-yay! It scares me, Father, not because it's so hard but because in a way it's almost too easy. It's easy and natural for me to get into the Public Relations Mode and to work a crowd. One of the sins that so easily entangles me is that of people-pleasing. I tend to give them what they want. But I know that that is not what you want, Lord. As we plan and prepare now for furlough, will you please cleanse me of unholy, manipulative motives? Please help me to see others as people who need a word from You, not as walking dollar signs. Help me to throw off anything that smacks of manipulation, for that totally hinders Your efforts to work through me. Please help Ellie and me to find the balance

between accurately presenting our needs and those
of Oaxaca, and being crass salesmen. Father, I pray
that this coming season of deputation will be one that
brings honor and glory to Your name!

As furlough time drew ever closer, God helped me to
work through my concerns of impure motives. However,
another related issue soon surfaced: *vanity.* Any woman who
has ever faced an upcoming class reunion will relate to my
worries on that score. After two years of enjoying more than
my fill of Mexican tacos, enchiladas and tamales, I worried
about my weight. I wanted to return to the home country
looking sleek and svelte, so I went on a diet for two months.
By the time we left Oaxaca, I was feeling better about my
weight, but still fretted over my hair and my wardrobe. I
dreaded looking like the stereotypical dowdy missionary
lady. Vanity, thy name is woman!

We finally set out on our long journey north, but we were
beset by car troubles all along the way. We were frequently
forced to stop in extreme July heat to let the radiators cool
down, and I didn't handle the delays very well. I found
myself repeatedly dissolving into tears with no provocation
except the heat and the travel fatigue.

The last straw was Texas—it just goes on forever! On
our fifth day of driving, we were *still* in Texas and I was sick
of it. It didn't help that we had broken down again in the
middle of the Texas desert on our twentieth wedding anni-
versary. Instead of a lovely candlelit dinner, Ellie had the
truck towed into a town at 10 p.m., and we all dined on Taco
Bell bean burritos. Ain't love grand?

A little surprise awaited us in Phoenix, Arizona. Some
friends of our friends were on vacation and had offered their
home for us to stay in for a few days. We were so exhausted,
that after our friends let us in the house and left, we all just
dropped. Our kids sprawled out on the carpet and on the

couches—and instantly fell asleep. Ellie and I at least made it as far as the master bedroom, and within seconds were also in a deliciously deep sleep.

A mere fifteen minutes later our son, Isaac, woke us up to say that the police were there! I opened my eyes to see two burly policemen standing in the bedroom doorway. I was so groggy with sleep that I just closed my eyes again, but Ellie jolted awake and jumped up to go talk to them in the kitchen.

It seems that the neighbors had reported two strange vehicles and some people with multiple children making themselves at home in this house. The officers wanted some reassurance that we were not simply squatters taking advantage of an empty house. They asked Ellie who owned the place, but Ellie didn't know! The owners were just generous friends of our friends and we didn't even know their names, Ellie explained.

I eventually got up and went to face the music with Ellie, and the cops continued to question us for about half an hour. Then they made some phone calls to confirm our story, chatted awhile longer, bid us good day and left. Thankfully, we had not been arrested, but our nap certainly had been. In retrospect, it was truly a funny situation, but oddly I reacted not with laughter, but with tears.

After escaping the 115° Arizona heat, it was a delight to reach the cool redwoods of California and then the Oregon coast. We were so enjoying the scenery that it never occurred to us that finding a place to stay might be a problem in a tourist town on a national holiday. Which is where we were: Coos Bay, Oregon, on the Fourth of July.

Sure enough, there was no room at the inn—not anywhere up and down the coast for hundreds of miles! No hotel, no camping spot, no church basement, nothing. After searching for hours, we finally pulled over to the side of the road at a little park, and just slept in the vehicles. It was horribly cramped and uncomfortable, and I don't want to talk about it anymore.

But God had one more major surprise up His sleeve before we even reached our furlough destination. Once again we had been granted a generous scholarship to the Cannon Beach Conference Center to rest up before hitting the deputation trail. I had been dreaming about Cannon Beach for months previous. But once there, the dream was overshadowed by a nagging question in my mind. *Could I be pregnant?*

Enjoying the beach that first afternoon, I was suddenly struck by a very familiar nausea. All week it stayed with me until there was no longer any doubt. Sure 'nuff, I was pregnant again, which at least would explain the buckets of hormonal tears all along the trip. Trouble was, to my way of thinking, furlough was the worst possible time to begin a pregnancy!

I wanted to be at the top of my game for this furlough. I definitely did *not* want to be nauseated! I wanted to minister to others from a position of strength, not weakness. I wanted to look good when we spoke at churches. What was the point of having gone through the deprivations of a diet if I was now going to get fat with the pregnancy?

God took all of these pride-based desires of mine, and did away with them in one fell swoop. For me, early pregnancy is inevitably a time of weakness, nausea, and weight gain. Not being able to cook that summer, I was forced to allow my sister, Shannie, to cook countless meals for my family. She joyfully ministered to us, but it was humiliating for me.

Also, instead of enthusiastically pounding the pavement and contacting potential supporters, I could only limply wave goodbye as Ellie set out alone. I felt guilty for not doing my part and embarrassed about how quickly I was gaining weight by eating every hour to try and ward off the nausea.

Besides all that, I was dreading having to face raised eyebrows when people found out that we were going to have another baby. Ellie and I believe that children are a blessing and that God will always provide for what He ordains.

However, I knew full well that not all of our friends and supporters would see it that way. If I have to deal with the disapproval of others, I'd much rather do it from about five or six thousand miles away!

In all of this, God reminded me that furlough is not about me. It is all about Him. If I can't exalt Jesus in my strength, then I must exalt Him in my weakness. I couldn't win the approval of others by looking good, or being productive, or conforming to their expectations. I had to simply allow God to provide more prayer and financial supporters for us while I was relatively sidelined. That way, I couldn't claim any credit for it, and *He* would get the glory! He had it all planned out, as usual.

Reverse culture shock is another unpleasant little wrinkle that returning missionaries often need to iron out. After being gone for two to four years, you may find yourself reacting against once familiar things in the home culture.

The aspect of our own culture that was the most difficult for me to adjust to was women's clothing styles. As a mother of teenage sons, I cringed to see some of what passes for acceptable feminine fashion in our society. We had only been out of the U.S. for two short years that first term, yet the rapid decline in modesty during that time really alarmed me! Most upsetting to me was seeing how many Christians went along with indecent fashion trends instead of holding to a higher standard.

I am ashamed to admit that my ungodly response was often to sit in judgment on fellow Christians. Instead of simply discerning this as an area of concern, in my heart I criticized Christian girls for wearing the offending styles. God had to rebuke me severely for my self-righteous, Pharisaical attitude. I don't have an answer for the problem of immodesty among Christians, but God showed me that the solution was *not* to condemn.

That first furlough time was indeed challenging, but I can honestly say that it was a season of experiencing God's amazing faithfulness in new ways. He supplied great housing situations for us, both in British Columbia and in Oregon. He provided good friends for all of our children, helping to take the edge off their homesickness for Mexico. He helped us accurately represent Oaxaca to friends and churches without feeling a conflict of interest. He heaped abundant blessings on our family, reassuring us of the love of our supporting friends.

Post-Pedestal Pondering

Yes, the furlough and deputation systems are admittedly flawed, but that is no obstacle to Almighty God! He still manages to teach, rebuke, correct, train, encourage, heal, and provide for His servants, even through faulty systems. If you are a missionary, you will face furlough frustrations. The challenge is for you to view furlough as more than just a trial to endure. If you are a spiritual leader based in the home country, your challenge is to understand the needs of your returning missionaries and be ready to minister to them.

All of us need to keep in mind that furlough:

- Can be exhausting (include a time to rest!)

- Tends to magnify insecurity (cling to the Rock!)

- Exposes unholy, manipulative motives (correct them!)

- Is a time to exalt Jesus (in our weakness and in our strength!)

- Can create reverse culture shock (guard against a critical spirit!)

- Is an opportunity to learn from the Master (learn your lessons well!)

There is a key to success when facing the challenges of furlough. The key is to learn not to exalt ourselves while representing the needs of our mission field. Purely and simply, it is to allow *Jesus* to be seen in and through us. That means being transparent, so that His work in us is not hidden. It means dispensing with the P.R., and sharing from our hearts. It means refusing to be nudged onto a pedestal — even for a moment — and continually crowning *Jesus* with glory and honor for all He has done!

CHAPTER FIFTEEN

Communicating Authenticity **or** *Clues for the News Blues*

Are we beginning to commend ourselves again?
Or do we need, like some people, letters of
recommendation to you or from you?
2 Corinthians 3:1

I sat out in the yard swatting flies, chewing on my pen, and doodling on my notebook. It was that time again... time to write the monthly newsletter, and my mind was a complete blank. The minutes ticked by. No inspiration came. No epiphany manifested itself. Finally, in frustration, I threw my pen down, and marched into the house to tackle an easier job—maybe scrubbing the floor or painting the house. Anything would be easier than this newsletter nightmare!

The task of sending out regular updates to home churches, friends, and supporters can at times be daunting to even the most seasoned of missionaries. Rookies can be paralyzed by the prospect. Pastors who are expected to come up with a monthly (or weekly!) letter to their congregation often face serious writer's block.

No doubt about it, it is just plain hard work to think of something positive and encouraging to write month after month. But while communicating regularly with your supporters or congregation may be tough, it is essential.

Pastors are seldom, even in the smallest of churches, able to stay in close contact with every person in their congregation. The pastoral letter serves the purpose of maintaining relationships, casting vision, encouraging the believers, correcting misconceptions, etc. Although sometimes difficult to learn how to handle, a regular letter to his congregation can be a vital tool in the pastor's hands.

Missionaries are, by definition, 'sent out' from one place to another. Often their prayer and financial support from the home base is dependent on their regular updates. It is a hard lesson to learn that a financial or spiritual slump will often follow hard on the heels of a letter-writing slump. That's just the nature of the beast. We need to be accountable to our home constituents, and geographical distance often demands written, rather than face-to-face reports. Obviously it is not an ideal situation, but it is the reality. What to do?

I don't have any brilliant solution to this communication challenge, but after twenty-plus years of writing regular newsletters, I have stumbled upon a few tips that might prove helpful to you.

Clue #1—At the risk of stating the obvious, my first order of business must be to pray! The newsletter update is an indispensable component to our ministry, and as such, is just as critical a target for Satan to attack as evangelism, personal devotions, or family life. Every writing project should be covered by God's protection in prayer. I will often compose a whole page of chicken scratch before I realize that it is just a lot of 'sound and fury, signifying nothing'. At that point, I remember to pray and ask the Holy Spirit to guide my writing. God is faithful, and the letter inevitably takes a turn for the better.

Clue #2—Another important thing that I try to remember is to avoid saying anything negative about my host country or authorities. I never know when one of my letters might wind up on the desk of some government official from Mexico, or when a traveling businessman from our area might happen to visit a church where one of our letters is posted on the bulletin board. Negative comments could spark a whole 'series of unfortunate events,' possibly even jeopardizing the presence or safety of mission agencies in Mexico.

A recent example is that of Pat Robertson suggesting that someone should assassinate the president of Venezuela. Result? The Venezuelan government is revoking visas and has issued a 90-day eviction notice to some American missionaries. Now obviously Pat Robertson is a high-profile leader, and not some obscure missionary from Smallsville, U.S.A., but the same principle holds true.

Nothing good and possibly much harm can be done by publishing negativity in a letter or broadcasting it from the pulpit. Even when sorely provoked by enigmatic foreign customs all around me, I must not criticize! Even when I am ready to scream with the frustration and discomfort of culture shock, I must not publicly attribute any blame to the country or customs of my host culture. Instead, I should try to find a close-at-hand confidante to whom I can vent until whatever culture shock or offense has passed and I have again learned how to cope.

Clue #3—Some mission agencies require their missionaries to submit their newsletters to a 'letter-checker' before sending them out. The letter-checker is usually a senior representative of the mission who scrutinizes each letter for any inappropriate content. This might be a good safety net to catch anything fishy in a letter, particularly for newly-assigned personnel who are still learning the ropes. Our wonderful mission, Missionary Ventures, does not currently require this of us, but whenever I am in doubt about something that I have written, I ask Jamie Loker, a Missionary Ventures friend and co-worker, to edit my letter.

Several years ago I experienced a miscarriage and then a D&C in a Oaxacan hospital. Afterwards, feeling very depressed and disappointed with God over the loss of the baby, I vented my feelings in an update to our supporters.

According to the premise of this book, which is the importance of living transparently before others, there was nothing wrong with what I wrote. However, it raised red flags in the mind of Jamie, who knows me very well. She discerned that I was feeling angry and bitter, and that I was just using the newsletter to host a little pity-party. She predicted that I would snap out of my "funk" within a few days, and so she vetoed my letter. I'm so glad that she did, because sure enough, a short time later I was feeling great, and would have deeply regretted whining about my hardships.

Clue #4—Wisdom sometimes dictates a slight delay in communicating bad news, at least until one is able to share without bitterness. On the other hand, I think that if I were struggling with on-going depression that was more than just a fleeting discouragement, the need for prayer support would definitely outweigh the danger of being perceived as a whiner. It's a fine line. Having a letter-checker who knows me well helps me to find the balance.

Clue #5—I have found that using humor in a letter can really help to ease the sting of bad news. After a run of bad health (including an appendectomy) last year, we were feeling pretty desperate down here in Oaxaca, and needed to rally our home constituents to prayer. Humor helped to communicate our situation without sounding quite so pathetic. Consider these excerpts from our newsletter last summer.

Caution: The following contains some material of questionable interest pertaining to health-related issues. Reader Discretion is advised...particularly if you find that people sharing about their endless ailments is about as fascinating to you as, say, cleaning toilets.

An explanation is in order. For the last two months, I have neglected writing the monthly update for one of four reasons. Take your pick: Sickness, Surgery, Service or Sinusitis. June and July were pretty much defined by the above four S's—sometimes overlapping—and now the Sinusitis one is leaking into August. It has been an interesting summer.

I think that using humor not only helped to cushion the impact of dreary news, but also helped to elicit a positive response as we begged for more prayer support.

Me? I'm still feeling perfectly yucky, and I just can't shake this sinusitis thing. Sorry to bore you with all these gory details of our health or lack thereof, but hey, we need some help here! As Ellie said yesterday, we are sick and tired of being sick and tired. We have prayed continually for healing, and have rebuked these attacks in spiritual warfare. But I gotta be honest here. We're feeling kind of worn down and beaten up by these unrelenting waves of illness. Even our dog is sick! Seriously. He has a big abscess on his head that just won't go away even with aggressive treatment. And now our car is sick, too!

So what's a missionary to do? Obviously I am not the type to suffer in silence, so that option is out. Instead we need to rally the troops in prayer. The purpose of this epistle is not to generate sympathy for our plight

(although we do like sympathy). It is really to beg you
to "hold up our arms in the battle" through prayer.

Clue #6—Sometimes when writer's block hits me, I just
start by describing my surroundings. Usually as I write, God
will use the description to prompt me in the right direction
for the rest of the letter. I wrote the following intros to letters
having no idea of what was going to come next.

*Twenty vultures are wheeling in slow circles over-
head as they make their way home to roost for the
night in our tall trees. I have another load of laundry
ready to hang out on the line (although it won't dry by
nightfall). Benjamin is outside chasing our chickens.
Caleb and Josh are tuning their guitars, getting ready
to go lead worship at the Mexican youth group. The
other kids are playing around here somewhere. I
can hear the bells ringing from the Catholic church
in town. This morning there were twelve other kids
here—besides our seven—some playing soccer and
fixing bikes and some dressing up and dancing to
waltzes with Johanna. Ellie worked half the day at
the recording studio. All in all it has been a typical
Saturday for us here in Mitla, Oaxaca, Mexico.*

(Three months later)

*We are at the peak of the hot season here in Mitla,
and let me tell you, it is! Other than going swimming,
I've found one of the best ways to deal with the heat is
to soak myself with water from a bucket and just walk
around with wet clothes all day. It works. Pragmatism
trumps elegance for this northern-born body of mine!
Not much used to semi-arid desert heat, we are all
anticipating the arrival of the rains next month.*

(Couple of years later)

It's a lazy Saturday afternoon. A front-hoe machine-thingy is outside digging up all the scrubby little trees and cacti in the desert beside our house. The land-owners tell me that they are going to plant hundreds of maguey plants –the big, spiky cactus-looking things from which Oaxacans brew their famous mezcal whiskey. You've heard of tequila with the worm in the bottle? Same thing with mezcal!

Speaking of worms, we seem to have a large family of tiny red worms living in our water cistern. Often I put a pot of water on to boil and have to fish a worm out first. It's not really that big of a deal, but it can be a bit disconcerting when you brush your teeth and spit out a worm!

Clue #7—Usually my letters take the form of a chatty letter to friends. Once in a while, however, I am inspired to vary the format. For example, a letter after our first furlough took on a Good News/ Bad News format.

Good News: We are all here in Oaxaca safe and sound. Praise the Lord!

The little girls and I boarded a plane... and ten days later our men arrived, having taken the long road with two vehicles and the cargo trailer.

Bad News: Ellie and the boys got only as far as Arizona before the van broke down. The mechanic was adamant that Ellie should not attempt to take that van into Mexico. It was dead. Let it lie. Problem: How does one buy a new van without enough money?

Good News: We went to prayer. Within two days, Ellie found a nice fifteen- passenger van, and thanks

to the quick response of some faithful friends, he and
the boys were back on the road home in no time.

Bad News: Just outside of Monterrey Mexico,
the leaf spring on the trailer broke! Things looked
bad, but...

Good News : It was just then that a Texan in a
pickup came by and told Ellie that there was a shop less
than a mile down the road that could help them. When
Ellie got there, the pickup was pulled over and flashing
its lights to indicate the exact spot. Come to find out,
it was a shop that specializes in fixing leaf springs! It
only cost twenty-five dollars and was then as good as
new. My thought is: Could that Texan have been an
angel? Do angels come with southern drawls?

Four months later, the news update looked different yet
again.

The Time:	*7:55 p.m., Thursday of Holy Week*
The Place:	*Town square in the mountain village of San Juan Mixtepec.*
The People:	*Ellie; the linguists who had translated the New Testament; the entire population of about 900 villagers; and two young ladies from the city of Miahuatlan.*
The Event:	*The showing of the second half of the Luke 'Jesus' video in the town square.*

*For the second night in a row, all 900 people of
the village had turned out en masse and were now
waiting patiently to watch the conclusion of the first
movie they had ever seen in their own language.
Ellie was stalling for time, playing some Spanish*

cartoons for the children and silently praying for a miracle. You see, the Luke video that everyone was waiting so expectantly to see was not there yet! The Christians in another town of the same language area had borrowed Part 2 to show to their people the night before. They had promised to send it on to San Juan on time for the showing at 8 o'clock. It had been dark for some time now, but the video had not arrived . Ellie and the linguists and pastor were tempted to just show the Spanish version of the movie instead, which most people would not have understood. Just at that moment, two girls shod in flimsy plastic sandals walked into town, up to the projector, and triumphantly handed the video to Ellie.

These two girls had been entrusted with the delivery of this valuable evangelism tool, and early in the day had started out by bus en route to San Juan. Unbeknownst to everyone concerned, the bus didn't go as far as San Juan on Thursdays. When it stopped at the next closest town and turned around, the girls simply got out and started walking. There was no way to call for help as the phone lines in both towns were out. So they just walked—for five hours on the dusty dirt mountain road—through dusk and into the night, without flashlights, going from an elevation of 2,000 to 8,000 feet, until they finally reached their goal! They were rewarded for their journey and blisters as the 900 people of San Juan Mixtepec sat in rapt attention, watching as the Gospel message was portrayed on the screen. Undoubtedly the Holy Spirit planted many seeds that night that will later spring to life and bear fruit. And all because of the beautiful feet upon the mountains of two young girls in plastic sandals!

Clue #8—Occasionally an obvious theme will present itself for the whole letter, such as this year's October update.

This is the week of the Day of the Dead here in Mitla, Oaxaca. If you are the typical Mitleño, you will be very busy this week preparing an enormous, elaborate altar in your home on which to offer sacrifices to all of your dead family members. From the market stalls lining the streets you will buy flowers, incense, candles, mezcal whiskey, cigarettes, toilet paper, and anything else that you think your relatives' spirits might need in the coming year. You will buy and give away many huge loaves of 'Dead Bread' with frosting skulls painted on them.

You will prepare special hot dishes of the best food to offer to your family's departed spirits as they drop in to eat on certain days. The spirits of babies who died before being baptized will show up on one day, dead baptized children the next day, and dead adults on the following. The church bells will ring and fireworks will explode all over town at twelve noon, signaling the arrival of the spirits for their meals.

You will also spend at least one all-night vigil in the cemetery this week, watching over the candle-lit, flower-festooned graves of your dear departed loved ones. All of this ritual will cost you big bucks—maybe even hundreds of dollars—for which you may have to plunge deeply into debt. It is costly, but you fear that failing to sacrifice will cost you even more in reprisals from the spirit world—your life or that of a family member within the next year. How can you take the chance?

This is the cultural climate of our town around All Saints' Day. The supposed veneration of the saints is really an attempt to appease the spirits, and behind all the festivities it is dark and fearful. 'Mitla' means 'Place of the Dead', yet in the midst of all this preoccupation with death, under the radar it is actually a 'birthing center'.

It is here in Mitla that fellow missionaries give birth to New Testament translations in blood, sweat and tears, having first been 'pregnant' for years while learning one of over 120 difficult indigenous languages. They also spend years in labor to make faithful translations of the scriptures and make them available for people to read.

For the many thousands of illiterate or semi-illiterate people here in Oaxaca, Ellie and the team of guys in the studio work with the linguists and native translators to record these New Testaments on cassettes and CDs. It is here that Ellie dubs the Luke 'Jesus' videos and the Genesis videos into the many indigenous languages of Oaxaca, making the gospel message accessible to those who cannot read.

In many ways, it is from here in Mitla that the light of God's Word is penetrating the spiritual darkness of Oaxaca and other Mexican states in order to dispel the fear of death and to birth the reality of new life in Jesus.

If you are not yet involved but would like to share in the thrill of birthing new believers for God's kingdom, please write to us. Besides our personal support needs, there are many other exciting ministry projects that need 'pro-birth/pro-life' investors. Or perhaps you are already supporting our 'midwifery ministry' here in Mitla. Your faithfulness and generosity are helping to transform a place of death into a bustling spiritual maternity ward! On behalf of those who have been reborn, we <u>thank you</u>.

(And no, I'm not pregnant again...I just like the birth analogy!)

Clue #9—Although as a rule I try to avoid whining in my letters, good old fashioned honesty is essential and appreciated. Keeping that in mind, I wrote the following while facing the imminent departure of our oldest son for college.

We find ourselves in a strange season of life right now—with a newborn baby, a son ready for college, and kids of every age in between! Caleb has been accepted at Patrick Henry College in Virginia and is planning to start this fall. He is hoping to go to Oregon to work this summer before college. We would really appreciate your prayers for him as he scrambles both to earn money for school, and to find any available scholarships. Pray for us, too! Although we have successfully deferred any serious 'empty nest syndrome' for years to come, it still hurts to have even one fledgling leave the nest. We need grace to say goodbye to Caleb in just over two months.

Then I addressed the situation again in a later letter, since the grief that I had gone through was very real and long-lasting. By honestly sharing my struggles, I was blessed by the supportive prayers of God's people pulling me through.

This has been a wild and wonderful couple of months as, with God's help, we have all adjusted to our shifting family profile. Thanks for your prayers for me especially as I grieved for two months prior to Caleb leaving. I am pleased to report that the anticipation of having the first chick fly the coop is actually worse than the reality. Now that Caleb is finally gone, I'm fine.

This last year has been a busy one for me as I have been teaching two Bible studies: one at the women's prison in Tlacolula, Oaxaca, and one to some Mexican ladies here in our town of Mitla. In our December letter, I shared some victories that we were experiencing in the prison ministry.

> *At the end of last week's study, Maria, one of the inmates, was telling us how she might be released sometime in this coming year. Then she commented, "But even if I'm not released, I'm already free in Jesus." That was Maria's first public confession of her faith in Christ, and we all rejoiced and cried with her. Please continue to pray for all of the ladies of the prison.*

Then, in the interests of honesty, I also included the following:

> *I would also appreciate your prayers for the Bible study that I teach to some Mexican ladies here in Mitla. I am supposed to finish up the last three lessons before Christmas, and these lessons are critically important—having to do with Jesus' death, burial, and resurrection. To be honest, though, I am really having a tough time staying motivated to press on to the end. I am tired, and it is tempting just to give up and quit now—especially when ladies say they will come and then don't show up. This is a very tangible spiritual battle, and I need your prayers to finish well.*

Clue #10—Every once in a while, when all else fails, and for the life of me I can't think of anything particularly edifying to report, I will just highlight some of our family activities as in this letter from last year.

And now for a sampling of 'Quezada Family Trivia' in no particular order of importance: Lydia (nine months) began crawling last week. Esther (four years) fell off a chair, cut her head, and needed three stitches. A stray donkey spent the morning grazing in our yard today. Benjamin (seven years) is missing various front teeth, and has a particularly charming grin these days. No more red worms in our water! Johanna (nine years) has recently turned into a jump-rope enthusiast. Isaac (eleven years) is excelling at piano and supplied the background music for a science and art exhibit last month. We are reading 'The Best Christmas Pageant Ever' as a bedtime story these days. Lucas (thirteen years) has suddenly shot up in height and is definitely going to leave his mum behind in the dust. Josh (seventeen years) is interested in a ministry/ career in Christian camping, and is looking into the Explore wilderness training program at Prairie Bible Institute with that in mind. Caleb had way too much fun at college this semester, but is ready to make a fresh start and buckle down to some serious studying come January. Ellie played football with a bunch of guys last Saturday and scored a touchdown and made two interceptions! (He's still the man*!)*

Clue #11—Another thing that I have found helpful is to restate frequently the purpose for which we are here in Oaxaca. I think that this paragraph from a letter written during our first term here achieved that.

Three days ago, a skateboarding friend of our son Joshua was hit by a dump truck and killed right out in front of our house. The death of this young man served to drive home to us the reality of a lost world passing into eternity without Christ. The young man

*who died spoke Spanish and could have read God's
Word in his own language if he had wanted to. But
many of the dying people of Oaxaca are monolin-
gual in one of over 120 different languages. They are
also illiterate and have no access to the Bible in their
language. Our ministry here is to help rectify that
terrible injustice by providing Oaxaqueños with the
Word of God in audio and visual form. With it, they
have the chance to come to know the Lord Jesus as
their Savior—even if they don't know how to read.*

Clue #12—Throughout the month I try to take note of
newsletter-worthy events as they happen. These could be
victories or defeats in ministry, prayer needs, cross-cultural
challenges, children's funny sayings, coworkers' accom-
plishments, or even weather patterns. Then when I sit down
to actually write the letter I make notes in the margin of the
paper about what I want to include somewhere (I'm sure that
there is a high-tech computerish version of making notes in
the margin, but I'll leave you to figure that one out). Margin
notes are how I remembered to include this excerpt from a
letter three years ago:

*Day before yesterday our homeschool schedule
was delayed because we woke up to an invasion of
ants in our kitchen, and it took four of us a full hour
to sweep, spray and burn them out before we could
even have breakfast! Never a dull moment in the
Quezada Family Academy.*

*Recently I assigned Lucas (11 years old) a Current
Events report— anything of national or international
significance. This is what he came up with (unedited):*

*"Not so long ago, a boy in Mexico got grounded
from going outside his property. His mother held
him responsible for being home late the night before*

he got grounded. The boy was simply waiting for a few of his friends to go to a couple games of volley-ball. On account of waiting too long for his friends, his mother mercilessly said three words: 'You're grounded tomorrow!' Please pray against child abuse in Mexico. The parents simply do it for the fun, and it's in Mexico because the law is not backed up. Thanks to everyone who prays."

Those of you who know Lucas will of course recognize him as the boy featured in the sad tale of child abuse in Mexico. I'd say he's well on his way to perfecting his writing skills in the prayer letter genre. Maybe God has a career in missions in store for him (or as a criminal lawyer adept at blaming society at large for all ills)!

Clue #13—Since I am notoriously bad at sending out thank-you notes, the monthly newsletter is a good reminder to me of all the many individuals and churches who support us. I look for creative ways to tell them each month how vitally important their prayers and financial contributions are to us. One month I wrote this:

We heard recently that 454 ground support personnel are required to keep an F-15 fighter jet in the air for just one hour! Every single one of those 454 is essential to the task. How much more so in God's kingdom where each member of the body of Christ has an essential part to play! You are the ground support personnel sending and equipping and providing for this F-15 family to inflict some heavy damage on Satan's territory here in Oaxaca. We are so very grateful for each prayer offered on our behalf, and for every dollar of financial support that keeps us in the air. May God give you His strength for the task!

When our youngest girls, Esther and Lydia, were four years and nine months respectively, they both contracted whooping-cough. That Christmas season was a terrible time for us as for weeks we waged war for our little girls' lives. Our supporters also fought the battle in prayer for us, and God heard and answered their prayers. I tried to express to them our gratitude:

> *They say that it takes a crisis to reveal what a team is made of. Well, let me just say that in this recent whooping cough crisis, you, our support and prayer team, really proved your mettle. We were so encouraged by your concern, letters, medical advice, and prayers. We truly felt God working through your prayers to buoy us up when we were sinking. Your financial support provided not just for the monthly basics but also for doctor visits, medicines, and sometimes store-bought food when I couldn't cook. You were there for us! It brings tears to my eyes even as I write this to think of your faithfulness and love to us. Please accept our heartfelt thanks.*

Post-Pedestal Pondering

If you as a pastor or missionary are feeling overwhelmed at the necessity of sending out regular reports or newsletters, take heart! Communicating authenticity to your supporters or congregation might be easier if you follow these simple *Clues for the News Blues:*

- Pray

- Avoid saying anything negative about your host country/denominational authorities

- Submit your newsletter to a Letter Checker for inappropriate content

- Try to strike the proper balance between gut-wrenching honesty and whining

- Use humor

- Describe your physical surroundings

- Occasionally vary the format. Be creative

- Sometimes use a common theme for the whole letter

- Honestly share about *ongoing* emotional struggles, times of exhaustion, etc

- When all else fails, talk about the family

- Restate the purpose of your mission/task frequently

- Make note of newsworthy events during the month and jot them down in the margin before you begin to write

- Always express gratitude to your supporters/congregation for their prayers and gifts

CHAPTER SIXTEEN

Nobody Here
But Us Chickens!

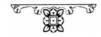

*Not that we are competent in ourselves to claim
anything for ourselves, but our
competence comes from God.*
2 Corinthians 3:5

We have all witnessed the glorious rise and shameful fall of many prominent men and women in Christian leadership. Each tragic incident supplies the enemies of Christ with additional fuel to make a mockery of Christianity. While the reasons for the sad demise of these leaders are undoubtedly many and varied, I am convinced that 'pedestalization' is one of the chief culprits. Leaders who are elevated to pedestal status often evade the safeguard of honest accountability to others. Without it, they are prone to hypocrisy. Once caught in the vicious cycle of trying to keep up a false image, it is very easy to succumb to serious temptation. The resulting fall is inevitable.

If we are honest with ourselves as Christian workers, we will admit that in spite of the hazards, part of us does desire to be up on a pedestal. Sure, it's lonely and cramped up there, but at least everyone looks up to you. Yes, everyone expects you to be able to leap tall buildings in a single bound, but it is kind of gratifying to be held in such high esteem. So we see that there is a tension between the desire to be on a pedestal and the desire *not* to be on a pedestal.

I spoke to one pastor who admitted that in a way he would like to be the pope. I understood what he meant. It would be so easy if Protestant congregations would receive their pastors' preaching with the same kind of respect that Catholic congregations give to a papal decree.

The truth, though, is that apart from Jesus, there is *no one* holy enough to live up on a pedestal—not you, not me, not the pope. All of us—leaders and lay Christians alike—stand equally in need of God's grace and forgiveness on a daily basis. We are all flawed and fallible human beings, and the sooner we admit it, the better off we will be.

The question remains, however: how real can a pastor afford to be with his congregation? Or a missionary with the people of his host culture? Or how about a missionary with his financial supporters back home?

As a pastor friend pointed out to me, "My congregation respects me for being a godly example to them. Unfortunately, according to their version of godliness, I am automatically assumed to be above the petty issues and ugly temptations that they themselves struggle with. How can I be honest about my temptations, doubts, and fears when I suspect they will think less of me for it?"

There is no easy answer, but I believe that a partial solution is to make the general Christian public aware that Christian service is for chickens. Now pay attention: I did *not* say that it's for the birds—I said that it is for chickens. You and I are well aware of the fears that assail us on a regular basis: fear of failure, fear of success, fear of people, fear of false motives, fear of inadequacy, fear of losing someone we love, fear of lack of faith—the list goes on and on. These fears can be crippling, though none of them are atypical to Homo sapiens.

We are not in ministry because we are inhuman robots impervious to pain and doubt and fear. We are in ministry because at heart we are chickens... but we have come to know Jesus, who sets us free from our fears. We are in ministry because we fear God more than we fear our fears. We are in ministry because we want others to know the One who has *conquered* sin and fear and death.

With such a One at our side, why should we fear diving off the pedestal? Why should we be afraid to be honest about our struggles? Or, to put it another way, "If God be for us, who can be against us?"

I recently heard Tami Milligan say at a women's conference that if you're going to share and bless people, you have to get naked. Obviously she was not advocating literal nudity as a ministry, but she was exhorting us to be open and transparent with others. She compared a sin-guarded heart to someone sitting on the lid of a trash can, trying desperately to keep the ugly stuff from bubbling up. What a great picture of the hypocrisy that pedestal living tends to breed among Christian workers! There we are, just white-knuckling it to be good, so that no one will see who we really are.

Why go through such agony? Why not instead admit your sins and your failures? Admit that you're a chicken whom Almighty God is pleased to empower for His service. It's not you, it's Him! Anything good that happens as a result of your ministry is not because of you, but because of the Holy Spirit in you. Admit it! Don't pretend. Don't hide your warts. Be a transparent disciple of Christ, modeling authenticity to the people you serve. When you hurt, don't hide your tears. When you're tempted, ask for prayer, and find someone to be accountable to. When you sin, `fess up.

Moses had the amazing privilege of being in the presence of God's glory. When he came down from the mountain, the Israelites could hardly gaze at him because of the reflected radiance on his face. In a futile attempt to prevent the people from realizing that the radiance was gradually fading away, Moses covered his face with a veil. He felt a very human desire to linger for a while at the table of others' awestruck admiration.

Knowing the criticism of his leadership that he endured, we can easily understand and forgive Moses his desire to prolong the pedestal period. But we must realize that it is entirely unhealthy to indulge in that desire ourselves. Nor is it necessary for us to obscure the truth. As ministers of a new covenant, we should exult in the freedom of transparency!

> *"And we, who with unveiled faces all reflect the Lord's glory, are being transformed into his likeness with ever-increasing glory, which comes from the Lord, who is the Spirit."* 2 Corinthians 3:18

I have a dear missionary friend who once shared from the pulpit at his home church about all the spiritual attacks he and his family had endured during their last term on the field. So devastated was he by the damage the enemy had inflicted that my friend actually dreaded returning to his assignment. Unable to maintain the pedestal posture usually reserved for guest speakers, he dissolved in a puddle of tears, begging his supporters to pray for him. The congregation was so touched by his transparent show of despair that they committed themselves to more earnest prayer for those battling on the mission field. Years later the church still remembers that as a watershed moment in their understanding of missionary service.

In contrast to *purposefully* diving off a pedestal through honesty, falling off a pedestal is a nasty business for all concerned. Both the one who is dashed against the rocks, and the people witnessing the fall are damaged in the process.

Don't let that happen to you! Guard against being placed up on a pedestal. You can continually remind yourself that you don't belong up there as you express to others your neediness before God, your tendency to blow it, and your sometimes-false motives. Gradually people will begin to see that you are just like them. They will resist the temptation to elevate you as they recognize that their spiritual leader is not perfect. That's okay, because their *God* is!

If you are already a victim of pedestalization, then dare to jump off now into the ultimately safer waters of honesty and authenticity. It is way too slippery up on top. Dive off before you fall off! The dive might feel scary, but humility is the only way to go. Come on in...the water's fine!

If we would all commit to a ministry lifestyle of transparency and vulnerability, we would see a dramatic reduction in the number of casualties who wash up against the rocks. When would-be worshipers come looking for candidates to pedestalize, we will in all honesty be able to tell them, "Ain't nobody here but us chickens!"

Epilogue

A friend recently exhorted me to conclude this book properly, and not just 'peter out' without telling you the end of the story. But therein lies the rub... because the story is not over yet. I am still living and breathing and learning. My family prefers me in this state (I think), so rather than tell you the *end*, I will simply update you to the present.

Except for Chapter Fifteen, I wrote this entire book while we were on furlough in B.C. and Oregon. At the time I was pregnant with our little 'unknown entity', who turned out to be Lydia Joy. She was born here in Oaxaca almost two years ago, and she is a hilarious little bundle of confusion, oblivious as to whether she is speaking English, Spanish, or some mysterious nether language in between.

Just three months after Lydia's birth, big brother Caleb flew the coop to Patrick Henry College in Virginia. While it was hard to see him go so far away, we were all comforted knowing that PHC was God's destination for him. Caleb is majoring in journalism and is now courting a lovely girl who makes him smile and who inspires him to be more of a man of God.

Meanwhile, back in Oaxaca, life for most people seems to be slow and relaxed...just as it *should* be 'south of the border, down Mexico way'. For us, however, it seems to rush past at a breakneck speed that keeps us gasping. Our ministry here is usually fun, always challenging, and some-times overwhelming in its intensity. It is definitely beyond our ability to carry out in our own strength!

Ellie continues his work in the recording studio—a five-minute walk across the desert from our house. His chal-lenge is to make the translated scriptures available in audio and visual format for the more than 120 indigenous people groups of Oaxaca. It is a *mammoth* task that Ellie will never finish in his lifetime, but we look forward to seeing how God will raise up more laborers to work in this corner of His harvest field.

Three or four (or five or six!) times a year, we host visiting short-term missions teams who come both to bless and to be blessed by Oaxaca. Our mission, Missionary Ventures, has a strong emphasis on short-term teams, having seen hundreds of people catch a permanent 'missions bug' through an initial week-long exposure. We are privileged to facilitate this epidemic, enjoying each visiting team. Some come to build, some to pray, and some to evangelize...but we pray that each experience will be contagious!

During this past year God broke my heart through my involvement at the women's prison nearby. As I was teaching a 36-week evangelistic Bible-study, the inmates somehow wormed their way into my affections, never to wriggle out again. Although the ladies have graduated from the Bible course, and I have announced my decision not to teach another series right now, I find that I can't just leave them alone. My co-laborers and I agree that the inmates' lives are too tragic and too lonely for us to abandon them now. Between us, we are committed to trying to visit them every other week or so.

While the other Bible-study that I taught this past year was not as emotionally draining, it was equally demanding

in terms of time. The ladies who attended represented a fascinating blend of Mexican and Zapotec cultures. Although two
of them made first-time decisions to follow Jesus, at their
graduation I also had to let them go. It was a real test of my
obedience to surrender them to God and to the hopeful, but
unproven, follow-up care of local churches.

The countdown has now begun towards our next
furlough beginning in less than three months. Through my
husband, the Holy Spirit has confirmed to me that I must
severely curtail my involvement in outside projects for now.
Preparing for furlough becomes almost all consuming from
here on out. It is a bit daunting to consider all that must be
done before we actually leave.

Our son Josh has to finish his senior year of high-school
(Grade Twelve for all my fellow Canadians out there), complete
with all the requisite college and scholarship applications. He
hopes to attend Prairie Bible Institute in Alberta, beginning
with their one-year wilderness 'Explore' program and working
towards a four-year ministry degree in Christian camping.

The younger kids are pushing ahead in their studies but
have a lot of work to do before we leave, including piano
practice, recitals, and exams. I also need to help them brush
up on their 'furlough manners', including, but not limited to:
chewing with mouths closed, remembering to say please and
thank you, and smiling when meeting someone new. Lydia is
begging to be potty-trained—a task that I completely forget
how to teach from one baby to the next.

We must prepare our Power-Point presentations for churches,
gifts for supporters, ministry brochures, and deputation itiner-
aries. In fact, there are a *myriad* of tasks to be done—tasks that
all point towards another exciting era in our lives: a four-month
furlough and then the next term back here in Oaxaca.

Of course we cannot know what adventures await us just
around the next bend in the road, but our lives are in God's

hands. *He* knows, and "…he is able to guard what I have entrusted to him for that day". (2 Timothy 1:12)

Thank you for sharing this journey with me!

To be continued…

Printed in the United States
53365LVS00003B/175-1011